BEYOND
THE MINARETS

BEYOND THE MINARETS

A BIOGRAPHY OF HENRY MARTYN

KELLSYE M. FINNIE

Foreword by Bishop Dehqani-Tafti

CHRISTIAN • LITERATURE • CRUSADE
Fort Washington, Pennsylvania 19034

CHRISTIAN LITERATURE CRUSADE

U.S.A.
P.O. Box 1449, Fort Washington, PA 19034

BRITAIN
51 The Dean, Alresford, Hants SO24 9BJ

AUSTRALIA
P.O. Box 91, Pennant Hills N.S.W. 2120

NEW ZEALAND
P.O. Box 1203, Palmerston North

ISBN 0 87508 969 0

Cover Photo: SuperStock

PRINTED IN THE U.S.A.

CONTENTS

FOREWORD

R eading biographies is one of the best ways of strengthening our faith and receiving purpose and vision in life. Situations change from one generation to another, but principles remain the same. Things were very different when Henry Martyn sailed for India as a minister of the gospel during the last century; however, the obligation for Christians to witness for Christ through total commitment and being prepared to pay the price for one's faith at any time remains the same today.

The life of Henry Martyn and his untimely death have influenced many people throughout the world. For one year he lived in the city of Shiraz, a center of learning and religion. Here he tried to share his faith with Muslim priests and to understand their points of view. Others who have attempted any serious religious dialogue with Iranian Shi'ite leaders will realize how difficult this task is. Suspicion and contempt can form antagonizing barriers between faiths, often expressed by aggression.

The story goes that while making a point during a religious discussion, Henry Martyn was met with verbal abuse about Christ; this brought tears to his eyes. Everyone was filled with amazement to see his non-aggressive reaction and the depth of his love for his Master. This affected them far more deeply than any intellectual arguments.

There have been several attempts by various scholars to write about the life of this humble servant of his Lord and genius of the faith. Without his tireless efforts the church in Iran would probably not have taken root, and people like myself might not have become Christians.

I have the pleasure of recommending this sensitive biography of Henry Martyn by Mrs. Kellsye Finnie to everyone—especially young people in search of a meaning in life.

H. B. DEHQANI-TAFTI

Former President-Bishop of the Church in Jerusalem and the Middle East (1976-1986), and Bishop in Iran.

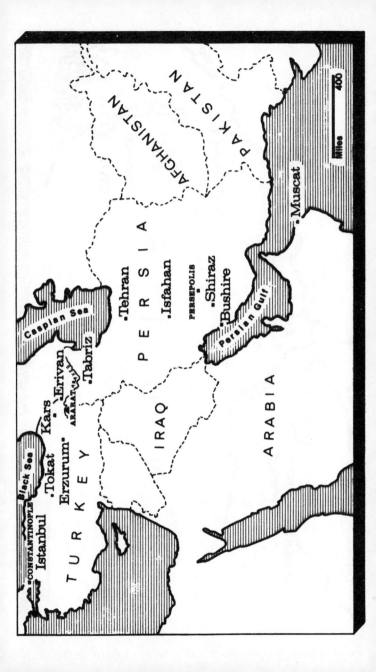

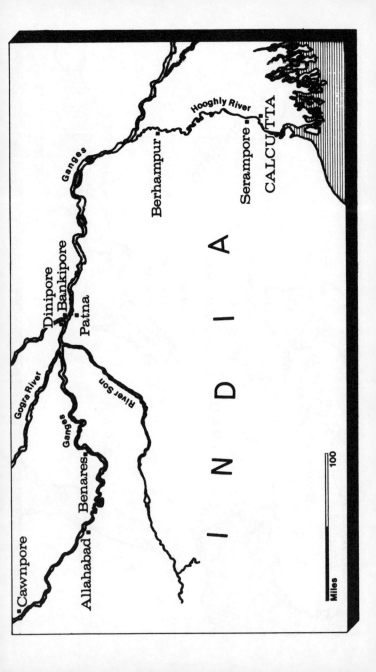

CHAPTER 1

A CORNISH BOY

His face alight with excitement, the small boy raced along—trying to keep up with the soldiers marching over the cobbled streets of Truro, his Cornish hometown. He knew that, as usual, his young sister would be trailing somewhere behind him, but this time he did not dare wait for her or he would lose sight of the marchers.

The usually quiet city of Truro was alive on this August morning in 1789, for it was filled with soldiers waiting for the noisy protest march of the desperate tin miners. The miners were on their way over the rolling hills to demand the higher wages they needed to survive.

"Henry! Wait for me, Henry!" Above the clatter of the marching soldiers the boy could hear his sister calling. Suddenly there was a loud wail indicating all too clearly that she had fallen. He stopped.

A hot anger surged up within him, for he knew he would have to go back to her. Now all thought of keeping up with the soldiers was gone, and soon he would lose sight of them completely.

Scowling darkly, he walked back to the crying child. But when he saw her distress the storm within him vanished as quickly as it had come, and his thin, plain face lit up with brotherly tenderness.

"Never mind, Sally." He picked her up from the ground. "Don't cry. I've come back for you." Carefully he took from his pocket a small periwinkle shell. "I'll wait for you, and here, look at my new shell that I found this morning by the water. If you stop crying I'll give it to you. You can have it for keeps, Sally."

This caring concern for his small sister had become natural to Henry Martyn, since for the last six of his eight years there had been no mother to offer comfort when needed. The two youngest children of the family had drawn close in a bond that was to last their whole lifetime.

The noise and the shouting of the protest march did not last long. When the excitement was over, the city soon returned to its normal remoteness beside the Fal estuary— to its peaceful fishing and the sound of the curlew over the water.

In France, just across the sea, the stormy Revolution was breaking out. But few of Truro's citizens had traveled far outside its boundaries, and news of the outside world was brought to them mostly by the arrival of the stagecoach.

This was a time when in Britain that outside world was one of harsh justice, particularly for the petty criminal—the death sentence could be passed on a young person for stealing five shillings from a shop, cutting down a tree in any avenue, or even for impersonating a Chelsea Pensioner!

Not surprisingly the prisons had become more and more crowded and had begun to burst at the seams. Something had to be done, and Britain, more eager to build up her Empire abroad than to deal with trouble at home, decided to rid herself of "undesirable characters." This was done by shipping boatloads of convicts over to the other side of the world.

Australia, discovered some years earlier by Captain Cook, was thought to be a suitable destination for these miserable sinners, and transportation had begun with the first fleet sailing from Portsmouth in 1787.

However, the influence of men such as the preachers Wesley and Whitefield, Wilberforce with his anti-slavery ideals, and many other good men, was penetrating the conscience of the country. Guy's and other hospitals were founded in London, charity schools were opened, and Robert Raikes had opened his Sunday schools in 1780. Here children were being taught to read by easy methods based on light theology, chiefly by recitation. "A is for angel who praises the Lord; B is for Bible, His most holy Word. . . ."

This was the background against which the young Henry had been brought up by his twice-widowed father, John Martyn. This gentle but enthusiastic Nonconformist was anxious that his children should learn to appreciate spiritual values as they grew.

John Martyn was an intelligent man of business, a self-taught mathematician. He held the position of chief clerk to Thomas Daniell, local merchant and mine-owner, and the Martyns lived comfortably in a house looking out over the estuary. On the opposite side of the road was the Coinage Hall where Wesley sometimes came to preach; the glad sound of the rousing services echoed round the area. The hymns Wesley introduced in his meetings became the tunes whistled by the family in the house across the way.

In 1789 the family consisted of a son, John, by the first marriage, and from the second, the three children who had survived infancy: Laura was two years older than Henry, and Sally a year younger than he was. There is no record of any female relative or housekeeper in the home to take the place of the mother who had died soon after Sally was born. The father, who was devoted to his young children, managed their upbringing on his own. But this lack of feminine influence in the home was a serious loss to the sensitive, inward-looking younger boy, who had so much affection to give.

John Martyn was quick to realize that his son showed unusual scholastic promise, and when Henry was seven his father entered him at Truro Grammar School.

In those days the standard curriculum at grammar schools was of a severely classical nature, and Henry would be given a good grounding in Latin and Greek. Mathematics, in which he was to specialize later, was not added to the school curriculum until about 1805.

The Headmaster, Dr. Cardew, noticed that the small, nervous boy with the ready answers was being teased and tormented by bigger pupils, who enjoyed watching him get into a bitter rage. He decided to put an end to this trouble by placing Henry in the special charge of a senior named Kempthorne, a kind and popular member of the school. Under his protection the new boy overcame many of his fears and gradually his friendly, cheerful spirit returned.

Although unusually bright, Henry was not at that time particularly studious in school but often trusted to his quick wits to see him through.

By the time he was fifteen he had done so well that his father and Dr. Cardew suggested he enter for a scholarship to Corpus Christi College, Oxford. He agreed to do this and, young as he was for such an ordeal, traveled by coach to Oxford completely alone.

He was not successful in winning the scholarship and continued his education at Truro for one more year, his father still keeping before him the ultimate goal of a university career. While he was still at school the war with France became a certainty, drawing all Europe into a bitter struggle, and this continued during the whole of his life.

CHAPTER 2

CAMBRIDGE STUDENT

By the time Henry was finishing at school, Kempthorne, Henry's friend and something of a hero-figure, had entered St. John's College, Cambridge, where records show he was excelling in mathematics. Whether this influenced Henry is not known but, with encouragement from his father, he became convinced that mathematics was an important subject to study. In October 1797, Henry followed Kempthorne's example and became a student at St. John's.

Coming from the remoteness of Cornwall, Henry felt himself to be in a new world. He was quick to appreciate the beauty of Cambridge, with its many small streets inviting the inquisitive to explore. He walked by the calm waters of the river, his mind filled with thoughts of the new life facing him. He admired the stately austerity of the College building with its richly decorated gateway topped by the figure of St. John.

Henry listened with delight to the music of King's College chapel and, perhaps with less pleasure, to the constant buzz of conversation from fellow students. But more than anything, this was the place of learning, of adventure into new fields of thought and ideas, and his eager mind was anticipating this.

At first his studies proved a disappointment. His tutor found the undersized youth something of an enigma, for although he had a good knowledge of the classics, he was completely unable to "make anything of even the First Proposition of Euclid." And, after all, mathematics was the subject he had come to study.

After a time of struggling, the tutor asked a second-year man named Shepherd to see if he could help Henry to get started. Shepherd invited him to his room and study commenced, but all efforts appeared to be in vain. Henry became so disappointed over his lack of ability to get a grasp of the subject that in despair he was ready to give up and return home to Cornwall.

He had already packed when Shepherd called at his room to try to persuade him to stay on and give the lessons one more chance. This gave a boost to Henry's confidence and he agreed to have another go. From then on it seemed that gradually the problems began to straighten out, and at last comprehension of basic mathematical principles began to dawn. Once over the first hurdle Henry went from strength to strength, at last passing everyone on his way to the top.

This early encouragement to persevere was to become a formative characteristic of his later years, pursued—even against the advice of others—to the tragedy of his early death.

But life at Cambridge was not to be all smooth sailing. Henry was of course still an immature teenager, living away from home for the first time. He was torn by emotional problems, ambitions, fears and frustrations, and was liable to fly off the handle in a sudden rage.

In the dining hall one day an argument developed between two or three students. It was a trivial matter and could have been settled in a few minutes, but Henry's temper was roused. The others tended to laugh at his angry outbursts and this was something his intense nature could not stand. Suddenly he picked up a knife from the table and hurled it.

Fortunately his aim was as erratic as his temper and the knife missed its intended target, wedging itself in the opposite wall. With shocked surprise the laughter ceased and the meal continued in subdued silence.

Most of the time Henry's more usual attitude, gentle, courteous and kind, gave little indication of the storms within. For his many friends and those he loved he maintained a deep, warm affection.

Gradually he settled down to his studies with serious, dedicated application. At home there was his father, as eager as Henry to hear examination results as they came through. His sister Sally was more concerned for her brother's spiritual progress. Near at hand to guide and encourage was the dependable and trusted Kempthorne, who was not afraid to criticize if necessary.

At one stage, he thought Henry was too concerned with the praise of others and seemed to be studying chiefly with that in mind. "Shouldn't you also be doing it for the glory of God?" asked Kempthorne.

Henry listened politely to what he thought was strange and unnecessary advice, but paid little attention to it. Only later would he realize the importance and wisdom of his friend's good counsel.

CHAPTER 3

LEARNING NEW VALUES

During Henry's visit home in the summer of 1799 Sally often brought up the subject of religion, but he was not particularly interested in the subject, becoming irritated if she persisted.

"I spoke in the strongest language to my sister and often to my father if he happened to differ from my mind and will. What an example of patience and mildness he was, and I love now to think of his excellent qualities."

When October came Henry returned to Cambridge, leaving his father in good spirits, highly pleased at the academic success of his son. At the end of the year he was able to add to this by writing to tell his father that he had placed first in the examination.

Unfortunately, as it turned out, Henry decided to stay on at Cambridge for the Christmas vacation, knowing all was well at home. This would avoid the long coach journey to Cornwall—which was tedious enough in the summer, but hazardous in the bleak days of winter snow and ice.

He missed being with his own folks for the festive season and filled in the time with extra study. He was sitting alone in his room in the early days of the new century when a letter was brought to him. It was from his step-brother John, and the contents completely stunned him, telling as it did that his father, who had appeared to be in good health, had died suddenly.

For a long time he sat with the opened letter in his hand, unable to take in the full meaning. It was hard to believe it was true, and in desperate isolation he had to face the first great sorrow of his life.

Where could he find comfort? He remembered his neglected Bible. How many times he had promised Sally to read it, only to fail to do so once he had settled back into college life? Now he reached for his copy lying under a pile of books and began to read. No peace came with the words and he was turning to look for other reading when there was a knock on the door.

Kempthorne, that faithful friend, that link with home, had come to bring consolation; at his suggestion they read together helpful verses from the Scriptures. By the time his friend left, Henry had decided to study the Bible for himself, not only for comfort but as a guide for daily living.

"I began with the Acts, as being the most amusing, and when I was entertained with the narrative I found myself insensibly led to inquire more attentively into the doctrine of the Apostles."

As he read more he realized that his childhood memories of the teaching of the revivalists in Cornwall corresponded with what he was finding out for himself. He was not used to praying, and his first attempt was simply to thank God for sending Christ into the world.

Like William Carey, the great missionary pioneer, Henry had no sudden vision but had started on a gradual searching for God. As he read of the offer of mercy and for-giveness through Jesus Christ, he asked that this might be his experience. He found, not a doctrine, but a personal Saviour and Friend. Later evidence showed that Christ now held the central place as Lord of his life. Before the nineteenth century was through its first month, Henry was ready to commit that life to the claims of God. His natural characteristics were still there of course, and he remained for all time a man of intense emotions, moving quickly from the mountain top to the slough of despair. He could be enraptured by music or the beauties of nature, devas-tated by personal failure or weakness, but he was no longer dominated by his previous passions.

Henry now shared with Sally his spiritual awareness and they wrote long letters to one another, encouraging or, if necessary, criticizing. He had other Christian friends at Cambridge, but the chief leader along his Christian path was the famous preacher, the Rev. Charles Simeon of Holy Trinity Church in Cambridge, which Henry attended regularly.

Simeon was a fearless man of God and in his preaching was a vehement earnestness unusual at that time. The three-fold purpose of his preaching, he said, was "to humble the sinner; to exalt the Saviour; and to promote holiness."

The teaching of this gifted minister was one of the greatest blessings that came to Henry and it was to strengthen and fortify him to the end of his days. There developed a wealth of warmth and mutual admiration between them, each fully recognizing the other's qualities.

Simeon held what he called "Conversation Parties" for students, and here the tea-drinking was interspersed with discussion and fatherly advice, mostly on the subject of Christian living. It was here that Henry met John Sargeant, the man who became one of his closest friends and who probably understood the somewhat unpredictable Henry best of all.

By the end of the third year, the student

who had made a slow start at Cambridge had worked himself up to the first place in all his college examinations. When his finals came in January 1801, just before he was twenty, he maintained his high position as the mathematician of the year and gained the honored position of Senior Wrangler.

"I obtained my highest wishes but was surprised to find I had grasped a shadow." Perhaps he was thinking of those words of Kempthorne during his first year. "Shouldn't you be studying for the glory of God as well as for the praise of others?" From now on that was to be his chief aim.

To his fellow students Henry was something of an unknown quantity. He was a man who walked alone with his thoughts, sometimes serious to the point of aloofness, yet ever ready for courteous consideration of others. One of his colleagues wrote of him, "Notwithstanding his unassuming manners and almost childlike simplicity, Martyn was perhaps superior in mental capacity to any one of his day in the University."

In March 1802 Henry was chosen to be a Fellow of St. John's and gained first prize for his Latin essay.

For the long vacation in 1802 Henry went home to Cornwall to be given a hero's welcome. He spent an enjoyable holiday with relatives and friends, and he and Sally had long, interesting discussions on the things closest to the hearts of both. He had much time for private Bible study and quiet meditation, a blessed relief after a strenuous term at Cambridge. It was for him a memorable visit which left, he said afterwards, a fragrance on his mind.

CHAPTER 4

WIDER VISION

When Henry returned to Cambridge after the long vacation in 1802, his first visit was to the Rev. Charles Simeon, and over their many cups of tea the talk turned to the subject of missionaries. Simeon had been impressed by reading reports of William Carey, the Baptist minister and shoe cobbler who had sailed with his family for India in 1793. He spoke so glowingly of what Carey had already accomplished with his translation work that the younger man was captivated.

Henry walked back to his room that evening with his mind full of the need for more and more people to take the gospel of Jesus Christ to those who had not yet heard it—for more translators to follow the example of Carey and make it possible for the Bible to be available in every language.

He started to read books on David Brainerd,

that dedicated man who had preached to the North American Indians, wearing himself out in the service of God and finishing his earthly course at the early age of thirty-two. Henry longed for Brainerd's devotion to God and his holy living. "I read David Brainerd today and yesterday and find as usual my spirit greatly benefited by it. I long to be like him. Let me forget the world and be swallowed up in a desire to glorify God."

The influence of Simeon's teaching and the thought of Brainerd's life as a missionary filled his mind. Earnestly he prayed for more missionaries to carry on the work, until he began asking himself the arresting question: "Why not me?" Was it for this that God had given him a gift for languages? Was this what He was preparing him for?

At first the thought appalled him. He had hoped to make a career among the learned intellectuals of his day, to live and work in his beloved native country. He could not accept the challenge, for his fastidious spirit loved refinement and culture too much. He could not live in conditions that were repellent to him, traveling along rough and dangerous roads away from all comfort. It was too much to ask of him.

So he struggled for many hours and weeks. But before the end of the year he knew there was nothing he could do but accept the missionary call. "Lord, here I am, send me."

Henry's decision came like a thunderbolt to those who knew him. Some saw it as a waste of scholarship and a brilliant career. Sally, in true sisterly style, told him plainly he was too inexperienced and not suitable for such a project. Simeon saw it as a triumph of faith.

Henry himself was not sure what his plans for the future would be, for sometimes he felt drawn to China where there were not yet any Protestant missionaries. At other times it was the country of India that tugged at his heart.

Through it all he began to see that Sally was right when she said he was not yet ready for missionary work. The Christian fellowship he shared with Simeon served to reveal to him his own lack of spiritual growth and depth. His self-examination as usual was without mercy, and to help him clarify his thoughts he began to keep a journal.

"My object in making this journal is to accustom myself to self-examination and to give my experience a visible form, so as to leave a stronger impression on the memory and thus to improve my soul in holiness. For the review of such a lasting testimony will serve the double purpose of conviction and consolation."

Henry kept the journal faithfully to the end of his life, writing down an honest account of his thoughts and actions as he analyzed them daily, never feeling satisfied with his spiritual progress. Everything was recorded—especially his struggles and failures, unconscious as he was of the advances he was making in the Christian life. The journal showed the literary style of a good writer as it portrayed his self-analysis.

The journal was a private thing, not written for publication, but when after Henry's death it was eventually opened by his friends, they found an authentic record of the way in which this young Christian sought to discipline himself as he determined to follow Christ more closely. It remains for succeeding generations a treasure of great price.

CHAPTER 5

PREACHING PROBLEMS

The Rev. Charles Simeon was a dominant character, ever eager to emphasize to young Christian men the joy and privilege of entering the ordained ministry. Rightly or wrongly, he influenced Henry to consider this possibility. Maybe this was a mistake, for Henry, brilliant as he was in other ways, was never particularly suited to the duties of a parish priest. Although he developed an absorbing devotion to the "cure of souls" of every nation, his gift lay in personal contact rather than in preaching from a pulpit.

Without any strong conviction that God was leading him along the path, and keeping India and missionary work on the horizon, he was eventually persuaded to seek ordination. Apprehensive of the responsibilities this would bring, he found little joy in the ceremony when he was made a Deacon in Ely Cathedral. As he walked the sixteen miles back to Cambridge he could only feel ashamed of the unworthy self he was offering to God for what Simeon called "the transcendent excellence of the Christian ministry."

He was now curate to Simeon, and the following Sunday he was booked to preach in the village church attached to Holy Trinity. He had been given no theological college training, for in those days a candidate was left to his own devices to prepare himself as best he could. The only training in preaching he had was by listening to the sermons of Simeon and others. He spent a worrying week preparing for Lolworth's pulpit, but it was not a success. One member from the pew stayed after the service to suggest that Henry's missionary call was due to immature enthusiasm only, for he appeared not to be strong enough in mind or body for that sort of life.

The second week he felt more optimistic until he read over his written sermon. "I was chilled and frozen by the stupidity of it." But in the evening of that day he was more composed as he read the Prayer Book Service at Holy Trinity before Simeon preached. His depression returned when the congregation told him they had not been able to hear him and that his reading should be altogether more solemn!

For a young man who had recently achieved the highest success in his university, these setbacks were a blow to his pride. He had not anticipated this kind of failure and it was hard to take. With a certain amount of legitimate pride mixed with a desire for humility, Henry wrote honestly in his journal "I began to see for the first time that I must be content to take my place among men of second-rate ability."

As a member of Simeon's staff there were other duties for Henry to carry out, one of them being the work of visitation in the parish. Although he was of a compassionate and caring nature, he did not find himself equipped or suitable for this; still, he carried it out faithfully. Often he was appalled by his lack of interest in those he was ministering to and he would leave with the feeling that he had been no help to them at all. Yet he could write in his journal, "With my Bible in my hand, and Christ at my right hand, I can do all things. What though the whole world believe not, God abides true and my hope in Him shall be steadfast."

Apart from his clerical duties there was still time for other outlets. For three years he was examiner in the classics at St. John's College, but however busy he might be he was determined not to neglect the study of the Bible in ancient languages. For his own delight he read the Old Testament in Hebrew and the New Testament in Greek. His excellent memory helped him to learn much of Scripture by heart; this was to stand him in good stead later when he journeyed in the solitary places of the earth. He set himself to learn the Epistle to the Romans in Greek, and also studied Bengali and Arabic languages.

One friend thought he spent too long alone in his room, and complained that it was not necessary for a Christian to become so much of a recluse, neglecting social duties and deadening the fine feelings we should cultivate. "His amazing volubility left me unable to say anything, but I kept my temper pretty well."

Henry did not tell his critic that, in fact, since he had become a Christian his taste for painting, poetry and music had been intensified, refining his mind and making it more susceptible to the sublime and the beautiful.

CHAPTER 6

A PROBLEM SOLVED

Henry's mind was still set on missionary work, confident that God was calling him to India. He finally decided to offer himself to the recently formed Society for Missions to Africa and the East, which later became The Church Missionary Society.

This decision had not been easy and with it came the anguished realization of what it would mean, putting an end to his cherished dream of a scholastic career among the intellectuals of his day. He would be leaving all he held dear—his family, his friends, and his country. But having made up his mind he remained unshaken in his resolve to obey the command "Go and preach to all nations."

Then, out of the blue, came a plan-destroying problem. Henry learned of the sudden loss of the small fortune left to him by his father, which was his only means

of support. Sally was dependent on him
and he had to provide for her; but the al-
lowance the Society could be expected to
allocate would only be sufficient for his
own needs.

Now the doubts crept in. Was God not
calling him to missionary work after all?
He could see no clear way ahead and in
despair he confided to his friend, John
Sargeant, "The door to India seems to be
closing." Henry's friends, concerned at his
obvious disappointment, gathered round to
offer advice and eventually a new plan
was suggested.

Although the war with America had
ended the year after Henry was born, when
the States had gained their independence,
England's war with France was a continuing reality. But her Empire in India was
being strengthened and enlarged, and the
power of Great Britain on land and sea was
a force to be reckoned with.

The East India Company, founded by
Elizabeth the First's Charter of 1600, held a
monopoly on trade with the East Indies.
The Company had regiments of soldiers in
various parts of the Empire to guard their
interests. They must be kept ready for attack by Dutch and Portuguese rivals as well
as by world-wide pirates.

Their ships, built and manned for both
war and commerce, were used to transport
to Britain stocks of tea, coffee, spices and
rich silks from China and India.

The Company was known to be opposed to the idea of missionaries going to other lands to seek to convert the heathen— "leave them happy in their ignorance"— but there could be a way in which Henry could take advantage of their assistance.

The directors of the East India Company, maybe through the powerful preaching of Wesley, had for some time been concerned for the welfare of their soldiers across the sea. They realized the need for spiritual help and guidance for men serving in units far from their native land.

Charles Grant, Chairman of the Board of Directors, was at this time looking for dedicated men of evangelical faith to fill the positions of chaplains in their units in Bengal. They were offering a substantial salary for the job.

"Why not," said Henry's friends, "approach them and get to India that way?"

Henry listened to their suggestion but at first he was sceptical, doubting the wisdom or success of such a move. Was he suitable for such a position? He wanted to be a missionary, the work to which he felt God had first called him. His desire was to get among the people of India to talk to them of God's love. How could he do this if he were to be chaplain to one of England's regiments?

It was only after serious consideration of the matter that he finally decided that if this were the only way, he would be willing to accept it.

Interviews were arranged in London for prospective candidates and there were visits to India House. At Leadenhall Street Henry met Charles Grant, who put his name forward to the Board for consideration and indicated that he would hear from them in due time.

For the man born and bred a Cornish countryman, a visit to the London of the early nineteenth century was an exciting experience. Henry found it a new world and he availed himself of every opportunity to see as much as possible. Among other places he visited the British Museum, reveling in its proud exhibitions. He attended musical lectures, called on John Newton the hymnwriter, and in company with William Wilberforce went to the House of Commons to listen to the persuasive voice of William Pitt.

Henry was delighted to be invited to go with Charles Grant to stay at the home of Wilberforce, and as they journeyed there in the coach Grant talked of the India so prominent in both their minds.

The aspiring missionary heard that Bengali was the language most widely used, but that Hindustani, which included Arabic, Persian and Sanskrit words, was used in many areas. Immediately Henry, ever eager for more knowledge, decided there and then to study them all!

Dinner that evening in the home of

Wilberforce was a lively meal. The conversation ranged over a wide area and the youngest guest at the table listened spellbound. His university training had fitted him to take his place among these important men of high standing and intellect. He appreciated the value of their guidance as he waited for direction from the East India Company.

When at last he went to bed his mind was so overflowing with plans that sleep was impossible. India filled his whole horizon.

CHAPTER 7

COMFORT AND CONFLICT

It was good to be going home once more, Henry thought as he traveled to Cornwall, in July 1804. He was expecting this to be his last visit before sailing for India. Both his sisters were now married, Sally's husband being Mr. Pearson, vicar of Lamorran and St. Michael Penkevil, about five miles outside Truro. Her new home was open to the brother she was always so pleased to see.

The journey on the coach took several days and there was time for meditation, something Henry was always ready to indulge in, writing up his thoughts later in his journal. "Most dreadfully assailed by evil thoughts, but at the very height prayer prevailed and I was delivered. During the rest of the journey enjoyed great peace and a strong desire to live for Christ alone, forsaking marriage. . . ."

This was a definite step of renunciation for, as only Henry himself knew, he was already in love.

When they reached Plymouth he stayed for a few days with his cousin Tom Hitchin and his wife, Emma Grenfell, greatly enjoying their Christian hospitality.

Then he set off for Sally's home at Lamorran.

When the family greetings were over, news exchanged and commented on, Henry settled down to enjoy the peaceful setting, looking out with tired eyes through the window at the Cornish hills that had surrounded him in his childhood.

Gradually the hectic university life of learning and study faded into the background. He was a boy again, throwing pebbles over the Fal; listening to the exciting tales of the fisherfolk; finding a robin's nest; and on one well remembered day, seeing the soldiers marching through the streets of Truro.

He loved it all, and in a letter to a friend he wrote, "The scene is such as is to be frequently met with in this part of Cornwall. Below the house is an arm of the sea, flowing between the hills which are covered with woods. By the side of this water I walk in general in the evening, out of the reach of all sound but the rippling of the waves and the whistling of the curlew."

This was his first visit home since his

ordination and he was hoping to use his time for preaching in his native surroundings. His brother-in-law invited him to the pulpit of his two small churches, where Henry felt more at home than he had been at Lolworth.

His old church in Truro thought what they considered his Calvinist views to be too severe, and they declined to extend an invitation to him.

It was a novelty for Henry's family and friends to see him in the pulpit, and Sally, in particular, enjoyed her brother's sermons. He was encouraged by the fact that Laura, the sister who had previously shown little interest in spiritual matters, was "deeply affected" by his preaching, and he enjoyed a long talk with her on the things that matter.

"In the evening I walked by the waterside till late, having my heart full of praise to God for giving me such hopes of my sister."

But Henry's mind was on other things beside sisters. Talking with Emma Grenfell on his way home had revived a train of thought that persisted. The Grenfell family had long been friends of the Martyn family, and still living at home in Marazion, near Penzance, with her somewhat possessive mother, was Emma's sister, Lydia, five years older than Henry. And Henry loved Lydia. He must see her once more before he left England for good.

One morning he went over to Marazion

and called at the Grenfell house. After greeting the family he persuaded Lydia to walk with him through the country lanes, mentioning nothing of his feelings for her. But before he returned to Lamorran he realized Lydia had crept further into his heart.

The knowledge of this caused tumult within. He wanted to be faithful to his conviction that God had called him to a life of missionary work in India. He had accepted the call at a time when he felt marriage was not for him—before he had realized he was falling in love with Lydia. He could not ask her to share what must inevitably be a life of isolation and hardship in a foreign land, even supposing she returned his affection. One moment he was tormented with the idea of settling down with Lydia and the alluring prospect of a parish appointment here at home. The next moment he knew this was impossible; whatever the sacrifice, his call to India was clear.

During the night he wrestled with his conflicting thoughts and eventually, unable to sleep, he went out to walk in the garden, seeking the peace that eluded him. "I could think of nothing but her excellencies and spent two hours reasoning with my perverse heart."

With his usual concern for others Henry kept his sadness to himself and devoted the rest of his holiday to his sisters until it was time to return to Cambridge. Not expecting to see them again, he said goodbye to his friends.

He called again at the home of Tom and his wife at Plymouth, and Emma confided to him the secret that she knew his affection for her sister was not altogether one-sided. While this news could not help but thrill his heart, it made him at the same time even more sad.

Henry spent another day in London with Charles Grant before going back to Simeon in Cambridge "to preach the gospel to my fellow-creatures that they might obtain the salvation which is in Christ Jesus."

He wrote to Sally, "Pray that I may know something of humility. . . . How it smooths the furrows of care and gilds the dark path of life. It will make us kind, tenderhearted, affable, and enable us to do more for God and the gospel than the most fervent zeal without it."

Had he perhaps been reading "We are afflicted in every way, but not crushed; perplexed but not driven to despair" (2 Cor. 4:8, RSV)?

Determination to persevere and proceed along a difficult path, whatever the cost, proved to be a characteristic feature of Henry Martyn which, under God, resulted in his fine achievements.

In the meantime students, hearing that he was back in the district, were eager to contact him and make use of his well-known talents. Difficulty in mathematics perhaps? Help needed for one studying classics? Children for extra tutoring? They all came knocking on his door, and none of them were disappointed.

CHAPTER 8

ORDAINED PRIEST

When in January 1805 Henry heard from Grant that the chaplaincy with the East India Company had been granted and would soon be finalized, he wrote in his journal, "I could have been better pleased to have gone out as a missionary, poor as the Lord and his apostles." He was asked to be ready to sail during the month but this was not possible as he was not yet ordained as a priest. This could not take place until a candidate was twenty-four years old, so Henry had to wait until his next birthday, on February eighteenth.

He stayed on with Simeon as his curate, still caring for the small parish at Lolworth, encouraged continually by his long talks with Simeon at the end of the day. This great man was aware of the limitations and mistakes of his young friend but he loved him as a son. He slipped seeds of valuable advice into the fertile mind of the one who would soon be setting off into unknown paths. There were warnings about the danger of being drawn into situations where secular interests could hinder the spiritual work of evangelism. Simeon stressed the necessity of reaching out to Asians in their own language and culture. Henry listened, and remembered.

On one of his visits to London Henry met Dr. Gilchrist, a colleague of Carey in Calcutta, and was able to give valuable help with the subject of Hindustani. Little by little the new chaplain was gaining information and experience while he waited in the wings.

He was asked by the Rev. Richard Cecil to preach at St. George's Chapel in Bedford Row. "After I had preached, Mr. Cecil said a great deal to me on the necessity of gaining the attention of the people and speaking with more warmth and earnestness. I felt a little wounded at finding myself to have failed in so many things, yet I succeeded in coming down to the dust and received gladly the kind advice of wise friends."

On March 10, 1805 Henry was ordained as a priest in the Chapel Royal of St. James in London. He also received a degree of Bachelor of Divinity conferred upon him by mandate from the university. Now nothing remained to keep him in Cambridge. "I felt more persuaded of my call than ever."

The continuing war with France made it difficult to fix sailing dates. Napoleon, with his lust for power and dominions, constituted a real threat of invasion, and the ships might all be needed in home waters.

For this reason Henry was advised to live in London while waiting, so that he would be available as soon as a date could be decided on.

Eager now, as any young man would be, to get on with what he had concluded was to be his life's work, he could not help but find this further delay a tiresome necessity. Henry hurried to Cambridge for a short farewell visit to Simeon. "I supped with Simeon alone. He prayed before I went away and my heart was deeply moved." He went to Lolworth for the last time on Palm Sunday and in the evening preached to a large congregation in Trinity Church.

Like a swarm of bees the students gathered at Henry's lodgings early next morning, ready to accompany him right to the coach. As he looked back over the past seven years in this noble palace of learning where he had been taught so much, formed so many friendships and grown, unknowingly, in the ways of God, the morning mist came down over the river and the stately spires of Cambridge disappeared for all time from his sight.

The war situation, with reports of activity between the hostile fleets of France and Spain, kept Henry in London for a further three months. His official appointment as chaplain for the East India Company was confirmed on April 24, 1805, when he took the oath at India House.

He was given an interview at Lambeth Palace, where the Archbishop stressed the importance of the appointment and cordially wished the new chaplain every success.

Henry paid another visit to John Newton and they discussed the work Henry would be engaged in, the visitor adding that he might not live to see much fruit. "You will have a bird's eye view of it which will be better," was the wise reply.

"When I referred to the opposition I was likely to meet with he said he supposed Satan wouldn't love me for what I was about to do!" The old man prayed before Henry left, adding his own benediction. At last came the final preparation for departure, luggage packed and roped, and farewell parties with new and old friends in London. At one of these he met a fellow-student from Cambridge, Daniel Corrie, and was delighted to hear that he too expected to be going to India to serve Christ in that land.

On July eighth Henry left London and on his way to Portsmouth to board his ship, he called at the home of John Sargeant, his Cambridge friend who had recently married and was living in Sussex. The strain of the past weeks—waiting in uncertainty, the hectic round of farewells, and the preparation necessary for a completely new life as chaplain—had finally caught up with him. He had never been very robust, and as he was getting ready for bed that evening he collapsed. When he regained consciousness he was in much pain.

Henry confided details of this incident to his journal but, stoic that he was, he appears to have told no one else about it, for nobody seems to have been sufficiently perturbed by it to query his physical fitness for the life ahead. By the next day he was so far recovered that he could continue his journey to Portsmouth.

What a sight met him when he reached the quay! A whole fleet of ships, too numerous to count, lay at anchor, with only the hovering seagulls to indicate there was life aboard. A forest of tall masts swaying in the ocean breeze hid for the moment the distant skyline. And among this array of ships was The Union which was to carry Henry and the 59th Regiment to their base some 15,000 miles away.

Sailing date was still uncertain as the convoy hoped first to hear of Nelson's return from the West Indies before they left. Simeon and Sargeant with other friends had gathered in Portsmouth with a view to seeing Henry off, and together they settled down to wait.

For another week the ships dragged impatiently at their anchors and still Nelson did not return. So, early on July seventeenth there came signs of movement throughout the convoy and orders came for all ships to be cleared of their visitors. Simeon said goodbye to the pale young man he loved as a son, clasping his friend's hand in both of his, and the many farewells were over.

Across the noisy docks came the sound of clipped commands, the shouting of the crew working as a team, the crack of the sails as they snapped open into the wind, the clanking of chains. Finally came the lifting of the anchors and the firing of the gun signal by the Commodore.

One by one the wooden ships began to glide farther out toward the open sea to maneuver their position in the convoy, and the watching people on the quayside began to disperse.

It was a triumphant moment for Henry, at last to be actually on his way to the country he had been thinking of day and night for many weeks and months. It was true he was not going as a free missionary but as one under orders, but his whole being radiated praise for the way God was surely leading him to the land where he hoped to live and work to the end of his days.

At that moment the mountain top on which he stood was lofty, but the ship was not many miles out before the new chaplain was in need of prayer as much as any of his flock. He lay in his cabin in the depths of despair, homesick, Lydia-sick—and violently seasick!

CHAPTER 9

DELAY AT FALMOUTH

T he fleet kept fairly near the coastline
    as it moved slowly westward and two
days later Henry found himself looking out
on a familiar scene. They were anchoring
in Falmouth Harbor. Tantalizing thoughts
began to creep in, reminding him that his
sisters, Truro, his friends, and above all
Lydia were almost within reach—and yet so
far away.

The following day they learned that
Napoleon's invasion fleet had embarked
from Boulogne, bringing the possibility of
trouble from the French. The British convoy was likely to be held at Falmouth for
some time and shore leave was granted.
What could stop Henry from satisfying his
intense longing to see Lydia once more?

"But I dare not—let the Lord open the
way if it is His will," wrote Henry in his
journal. But as the days dragged on,

Henry's own will weakened until in desperation one morning he caught the early coach to Marazion, this time determined to declare his love.

The family was at breakfast when he arrived, startled at the sudden appearance of one they thought to be away on the high seas. Mrs. Grenfell may not have been too pleased to have this earnest missionary-minded young man back on her doorstep, for although her daughter had reached the age of thirty Mamma liked to think the apron strings were still tied!

Henry and Lydia spent most of the day together and, with a shy reticence, Henry told of his deep abiding love for her. He asked if she would be willing to come out to him in India, should it be God's will for them to be married. She was hesitant and would give him no firm answer, suggesting there were obstacles such as the shortness of time to decide. That was understandable; but there was a deeper reason for her indecision and this she did not reveal.

In the past Lydia had suffered a broken engagement and—foolishly perhaps—she was unwilling to enter into another marriage contract while her ex-fiancé remained unmarried. Had she been able to discuss this with Henry at the time, it is possible much heartbreak for both of them might have been spared.

Poor Henry! Perplexed and despondent he went back to his ship. Yet in his cabin that evening he could write "May the Lord give me grace to turn cheerfully to my proper work and business." And away in Marazion Lydia was confiding to her diary "May the Lord moderate the sorrows I feel at parting with so valuable and excellent a friend."

On Sunday the new chaplain preached on board The Union and tried out his stumbling Hindustani on the Indian crew but found little response. "How I long to know their language so that I can preach the gospel to them."

Rumors abounded on the ship. One was that they were to go to Ireland first and then on to the Cape of Good Hope; but for the time being they just stayed on where they were, anchored in Falmouth harbor. It was too tempting for Henry, who could not resist making several more visits to see Lydia although she was not always at home when he called.

She wrote her secrets in her diary. "I learn from our servant that he called and left a message that he would be here tomorrow. My future happiness and his, the glory of God, the peace of my dear mother—all are concerned in what may happen tomorrow."

But when the next day dawned the wind was blowing from the north and the fleet at last decided to sail. The signal gun was fired but the chaplain was nowhere to be found. When news of the preparation for sailing reached Marazion there was no time to be lost, and it had to be a curt and hasty farewell. In the flurry of the moment Lydia raised no objection to Henry's repeated suggestion that she would come to India, although she would not enter into any agreement.

A horse was made ready and Henry galloped away, his one thought now to reach Falmouth in time. His heart sank as he came in sight of the harbor and realized it was almost empty. But the anchor chains of The Union had fouled other lines and, mercifully for the harassed chaplain, this had delayed its departure with the rest of the fleet. With a thankful heart he scrambled aboard, careful not to let anyone know why he had been missing or where he had been.

The next morning the spire of St. Hilary's Church near Marazion was still visible and his thoughts flew to Lydia and their frantic parting. She had said, he remembered, "We had better go free." What had she meant? What had she meant? The one who filled Henry's mind as his ship carried him past the Cornish coast was writing in her diary: "My affections are engaged beyond recall. It is now fairly understood between us that he is free to marry where he is going and I shall often pray the Lord to find him a suitable partner." Not quite what Henry had in mind!

He had finally left England, his missionary vision dominant, his chaplaincy a means of realizing it. As his native land slipped farther and farther into the background, his one aim was to live for Christ in the place of his calling.

But while his highly-strung nature was tormented by the remembrance of all he had loved and lost, his merciless self-examination rebuked him for his lack of dedicated holiness.

CHAPTER 10

THE NEW CHAPLAIN

T he fleet went first to Ireland where the
invasion threat kept them for another
two weeks. On August 28, 1805, accompanied
by warships, they left the safety of Cork
Harbor for the wild waters of the Atlantic,
made more dangerous by the maneuvers
of the English and French navies leading
up to Nelson's victory at Trafalgar.

Henry was thankful to have a cabin to
himself and this was stacked high with his
books. They were his only companions, for
among the crowded decks he felt not only
friendless but a complete foreigner. He
was a "raw academic," taking his meals
with officers and cadets in the galley—
pleasant and orderly enough, but the talk
was all of regiments, war, and firearms.

He spent much of his time on deck, seasick
and cold in the howling wind that whipped
through the rigging. Troubled thoughts

plagued him, chasing through his mind with the pointed finger of condemnation. "The world has a hold upon my soul and the spiritual conflict is consequently dreadful."

They reached Funchal, capital of Madeira Island, on September twenty-ninth and left the rolling ship for four blissful days on "terra firma." To everyone he met on the island Henry talked about the Lord Jesus Christ, fearlessly disputing with those who put forward mistaken ideas. He also found time to write a letter to Emma in Plymouth: "God knows how dearly I love you and Lydia and Sally and all His saints in England, yet I bid you an everlasting farewell almost without a sigh." Not altogether complimentary perhaps but, while his courteous spirit shied from causing unnecessary offence, Henry's nature was too deeply serious for trivial pleasantries.

Another forty days passed before they reached Brazil and throughout the journey the chaplain continued his personal program of Bible study, prayer, meditation, and memorizing parts of Scripture. His duties included a weekly service when some two hundred soldiers came, but they were not very attentive to his preaching, finding his sermons difficult to take. They were too demanding, they said, and set too high a standard.

One young soldier confided to Henry that he had been a choirboy, and this was the chaplain's opportunity to enlist his co-operation by asking him to start singing sessions. Henry himself had a rich deep voice and the singing proved a great success.

"Where's the chaplain?" became the common question, for this one was every-where. Like a true shepherd he looked for his flock in every corner, below deck or on the gun deck, chatting with sailors among the hammocks or having an earnest conversation with a man working in the boatswain's berth. In the afternoons he would read to a small group of soldiers and their wives, introducing them to the delights of *Pilgrim's Progress* by John Bunyan. Often he would go quietly down the ladders to visit those who were ill in the cockpit, groping his way to where they lay in the dark, taking them water and nourishment for their bodies and an uplift for their souls.

The chaplain's uncompromising presence in the ship made its own impact, and although some were offended by his ruthless warning of judgment, there were others who decided to follow Christ whatever the cost. A cadet's officer named MacKenzie became a true friend, eager to discuss spiritual matters and to progress along the Christian path. A faithful few met often in Henry's cabin, learning from him some-thing of the hardships as well as the joys of discipleship.

In his leisure time, Henry continued the study of languages that were to fit him for missionary evangelism and tested out his vocabulary on the Lascar sailors. Constantly his prayer was for the setting up of Christ's kingdom in the world, never losing sight of the solemn responsibilities of his vocation, always longing for greater spirituality. He did not mind that one of his friends on the ship had said, "He is a good scholar but a poor orator."

CHAPTER 11

TRESPASSING IN BRAZIL

T he voyage was not without incident, and soon after passing the Equator the whole fleet came upon a dangerous reef of rocks. Horror-struck, they saw that two of the ships were lost; but miraculously the lookout man on The Union saw what was happening in time and acted quickly, saving the ship from tragedy. Soon they came in sight of South America, and while one of the army captains was having a heated argument with the chaplain—blaming God for giving him the nature he had—the fleet ran into Salvador.

Brazil, then a Portuguese colony, was made up of Brazilians, Portuguese, and colored slaves. It was a joy to the sea-weary Henry to mix with the friendly people with whom he was to spend the next sixteen days.

His curiosity for new scenery sent him exploring, and he wandered through an open gate before realizing it was the private approach to someone's house. The trespass turned out to be the introduction to a fascinating and pleasant interlude, for as he decided to withdraw the owners came out, wondering who this was in their garden. Henry apologized in French, explaining his mistake and the fact that he was a stranger just off one of the anchored ships. The details of his meeting with Señor and Señora Corre are given in diary form in his journal:

". . . I was very politely desired to sit down at a little table which was standing under a large space before the house like a verandah. They then brought me oranges and a small red acid fruit, the name of which I asked but cannot recollect. The young man sat opposite, conversing about Cambridge; he had been educated in a Portuguese University. Almost immediately, on finding I was of Cambridge, he invited me to come when I liked to his house. A slave, after bringing the fruit, was sent to gather three roses for me; the master then walked with me round the garden and showed me, among the rest, the coffee plant. When I left him he repeated his invitation. Thus did the Lord give his servant favor in the eyes of Antonio Joseph Corre."

"Nov. 14: Señor Antonio received me with the same cordiality; he begged me to dine with him. I was curious and attentive to observe the difference between the Portuguese manners and ours; there were but two plates laid on the table and the dinner consisted of a great number of small mixed dishes, following one another in quick succession but none of them very palatable. In the end of the evening we walked out to see his plantation; here everything possessed the charm of novelty. The grounds included two hills and a valley between them. The hills were covered with coconut trees, bananas, mangoes, orange and lemon trees, olives, coffee, chocolate and cotton plants, etc. In the valley was a large plantation of a shrub or tree bearing a cluster of small berries which he desired me to taste; I did and found it was pepper, lately introduced from Bavaria. . . . Slaves were walking about the grounds, watering the trees and turning up the earth. . . . At night I returned to the ship in one of the country boats, which are canoes made of a tree hollowed out and paddled by three men."

"Nov. 18: Went ashore at six o'clock and found that Señor Antonio had been waiting for me two hours. It being too late to go into the country I stayed at his house till dinner. . . At his father's house I was described to them as one who knew everything—Arabic, Persian, Greek, etc. and all stared at me as if I had been dropped from the skies."

"Nov. 23: In the afternoon I took leave of my kind friends, Señor and Señora Corre. They and the rest came out to the garden gate and continued looking till the winding of the road hid me from their sight. The poor slave Raymond who had attended me and carried my things burst into a flood of tears and when I parted from him he was going to kiss my feet; but I shook hands with him, much affected by such extraordinary kindness in people to whom I had been a total stranger till within a few days."

So could Henry win the friendship of both the uneducated and the scholarly, able to converse with each person at their own level, ever desirous of their spiritual welfare, pointing his hearer to the claims of the God he worshiped.

CHAPTER 12

BACK TO WORK

The last sixteen days had been beneficial to Henry in many ways, restoring as they did his old buoyant spirit. The trauma of leaving England (with the events leading up to it), combined with the loneliness he felt in the new life on board ship, had obscured for some time the brighter side of his character. Although given to melancholy self-criticism when alone, with his friends he always had a gracious charm and a readiness to share a joke; he was often bubbling over with wit and gaiety. And at Salvador he had walked among friends.

But now he had to return to the serious business of being the spiritual adviser to soldiers who would shortly be exposed to the horrors and dangers of war. They had been told that their object was the capture of the Cape of Good Hope, at that time a

Dutch colony. It was necessary for this to be retaken by the British in order to keep the sea route to the East open.

It took five weeks to reach the battle area, and as the calendar turned to 1806 the fleet anchored near Cape Town.

The 59th Regiment landed and on January eighth the fierce battle of Blaauberg was fought. There was a loss of almost a thousand men, most of them from the Dutch side.

As soon as the fighting ceased Henry was allowed to go on shore with a stretcher party and a doctor. The men did what they could for the many wounded, who were either lying around on the sand or in the group of farmhouses that had been hastily turned into a hospital.

The battle had raged for two days before the Dutch surrendered, and Henry found his time taken up with helping the wounded men and bringing what comfort he could. He was able to find lodgings in Cape Town and preached at the military hospital where he visited.

Appalled by his close contact with the result of warfare, he wrote, "I felt considerable pain at the enemy being obliged to give up everything to the victors. . . . I had rather be trampled upon than be the trampler."

His journal records more of his thoughts: "I prayed that the capture of the Cape might be ordered to the advancement of Christ's kingdom; and that England, while she sent the thunder of her arms to the distant regions of the globe, might not remain proud and ungodly at home, but might show herself great indeed by sending forth the ministers of her church to diffuse the gospel of peace."

During his month at Cape Town Henry longed to find some Christian fellowship and friendship. When at Cambridge he had heard of a Dutch missionary living in Cape Town and decided to try and find him. He knew that eighty-year-old Dr. Vanderkemp was an agent of the London Missionary Society, and at last he was able to locate his house. Henry received a warm welcome when he introduced himself and immediately Dr. Vanderkemp introduced his fellow missionary, Mr. Read.

"I was delighted beyond measure. Meeting these beloved brethren so filled me with joy and gratitude to God that I hardly knew what to do."

Henry spent most of his leisure time with the missionaries, joining them in their family worship. Sometimes they would sit at night in the open, with Table Mountain in the distance, and Henry would listen avidly to their account of the missionary work they were engaged in. Nothing could have done more to encourage him in the path he had chosen.

"Talking with Read on the beach, we spoke of the excellency of missionary work. The last time I stood on the shore with a friend, speaking on the same subject, was with Lydia at Marazion, and I mentioned her to Read. However, I felt not the slightest desire for marriage and often thank God for keeping me single."

When Henry wrote this, it may have been he was trying to convince himself that this was the case; the truth was that his love of Lydia was still as strong as ever.

In one of his talks with Vanderkemp before he left Cape Town, he asked the elderly missionary if he ever regretted spending his life as a missionary. Like a shot came the reply. "No. I wouldn't exchange my work for a kingdom." These were encouraging words for the one whose great longing was to get started on the missionary pathway.

On February fourth the fleet set off for Madras. Illness among the passengers, rough and stormy seas, increasing heat, and a shortage of food combined to make this part of the voyage the most difficult. But Henry was encouraged by the continuing fellowship of MacKenzie and a few others, who came to his cabin for prayer and Bible study.

They caught sight of land on April twenty-first and the following day reached Madras. Henry was intrigued by all he saw, eager to learn quickly all he could about the country he had thought of for so long.

As soon as Henry and his possessions were on shore he was surrounded by a great crowd of coolies, all eager to transport his luggage. They picked up one box after another, going off in all directions—and he was forced to run after them to stop the dispersion! Only when he had managed to get all his things together again was he able to get to the Customhouse; even then he was closely followed by four coolies, an umbrella-carrier, and a boy deemed a "waiting-man," who attached themselves to him without invitation. At dinner that night they were waited on by turbaned Asiatics.

"Now that I am actually treading on Indian ground, let me bless and adore my God for doing so much for me; and if I live, let me have come hither for some purpose."

As a change from Henry's constant study of Hindustani and Persian languages, he left his lodgings one night to go to see an Indian village, accompanied by his servant, Samees. On the main street there were about two hundred terraced houses and on the little, winding paths were a number of detached ones. "Here all was Indian—no vestige of anything European."

On Sunday Henry preached at Fort St. George before the Governor, who was so impressed he asked for a copy of the sermon.

CHAPTER 13

NEW FRIENDS

It was very hot as the ships left Madras and edged their way up the Hooghly River until they reached Calcutta.

The next day, May 16, 1806, Henry stepped ashore as soon as it was light and went to enquire for the East India Company's senior chaplain, David Brown. He was disappointed to find that the chaplain was not at his Calcutta address but was staying at his suburban home in Aldeen.

It was a poor welcome into a strange land for someone who had traveled 15,000 miles to get there. But arrival time for ships was so unpredictable that it was not possible to make arrangements beforehand.

After further enquiries Henry found someone who could direct him to the missionary base of William Carey, the Baptist translator who had been in India since 1793. The meeting of these two men must have been an emotional experience for them both, for it was through hearing of Carey's translation work that Henry had come. When he was a young ordinand drinking tea with Simeon in his rooms at Cambridge and listening to his host's story of William Carey, he had been first alerted to the needs of India and her people.

For Carey there was the thrill of not only receiving a visitor from England, but meeting one who had the same aspirations as he.

As they sat at breakfast, the two men, from different backgrounds but with similar literary gifts and evangelical fire, talked chiefly of missions and missionary outreach. Then after family worship with the servants, Carey went back to his study to continue translating with his pundit from the Sanskrit manuscript, leaving his guest to explore his new surroundings.

As soon as David Brown heard that Henry had arrived in Calcutta, he came to fetch the new chaplain to stay with him and his family at Aldeen. Mrs. Brown, always ready to make room for another guest at her large family table, soon made him feel at home.

The house was set in a mound of foliage; mango, bamboo and teak were growing in abundance in the hot climate. There was a large green lawn under the trees where the Brown family played and where their parents could relax.

Henry soon made friends with the children, for in their company he could be as a child—romping with them, playing "lions and tigers" on all fours, or carrying the smaller ones on his shoulder. "Here comes Uncle Henry," they would shout as soon as they saw him coming over the lawn; then there would be a race to reach him first. His merry laugh would mingle with their shouts of welcome that rang out over the treetops.

Mr. Brown realized that Henry would need a quiet place for study, and he prepared an ancient pagoda that stood near the river at the end of the garden as Henry's special sanctum. This one-time temple was a strange place; its vaulted cells and walls showing carvings of Hindu gods now echoed the prayers of this dedicated Christian who walked so near to the living God. Henry wrote, "I like my dwelling much. It is so retired and free from noise. It has so many recesses and cells that I can hardly find my way in and out."

Here he wrote out his sermons to preach first for David Brown and later to both his English congregation at the Old Mission and the New Church in Calcutta. His friends now began to hope he would stay on with them. When a serious attack of illness and high temperature put Henry out of action for many days, they were deeply concerned about his health. It was obvious he was not robust, and rather than the strenuous life as a chaplain in an inland army center, they felt that Calcutta was more suited to his particular ministry and linguistic gifts.

He was also in close touch by this time with what was known as "the Serampore trio"—Carey, Marshman and Ward—and ever the talk between them was of oriental languages and grammar. "Three such men so suited to one another and to their work are not to be found in the whole world." They too would have liked their new friend to stay and join them at Serampore, giving himself to the study of Urdu (Hindustani) and translation. The many kind suggestions for his future intrigued him: "I was perplexed and so excited I could get little sleep."

But as chaplain he was not a completely free agent, and his first duty was to the East India Company and the men of the regiment. He knew he must wait to hear where his posting would be.

Apart from that, he longed to get among the native people—to mix with them and learn something of their hopes and fears, their traditions and frustrations. He remembered the wise words of Simeon when he had stressed the necessity of reaching out to Asians in their own language and culture.

While Henry waited at Aldeen he set himself to continue more ardently than ever with his study of Urdu, Sanskrit, Arabic, and Persian. His zest for learning seemed endless and the Brahmin who was now helping him was usually the first to tire of the day's lesson!

On some days Henry went for tutoring in oriental writings to Fort William College, where Carey was now one of the professors.

But all study went by the board the day Henry heard that his old friend from Cambridge days, Daniel Corrie, had arrived at Calcutta. He too had come out to take up work as a chaplain, and there were lively scenes of joy when the two friends met. Corrie was later to become Bishop of Madras.

CHAPTER **14**

A LETTER FROM LYDIA

Ever since their abrupt parting at Marazion, Henry's thoughts had never been far from his beloved Lydia. Although he seemed to be resigned to the fact that she would never be his wife, he knew that his love for her would remain.

Before they had reached the end of the voyage he had, he imagined, come to terms with it, and he wrote a final farewell to her. "Never will you cease to be dear to me; still, the glory of God and the salvation of immortal souls is an object for which I can part with you."

It is difficult to understand Lydia and her vacillations. It would appear that, although she was a committed Christian, there was something of the nature of a coquette in her make-up. She certainly seemed to trifle with the affections of this man; but he was sufficiently naive not to realize it.

She had been willing to send him away to India without her; but as soon as he had gone she sent him a letter, to keep fresh in his mind the memory of the woman he had left behind. At this juncture one would like to have whispered to him, "Think no more of her, Henry. She will probably break your heart." But he would not have listened.

Henry's whole nature was filled with love, first to God and, next, fulfilling the second commandment, loving his neighbor as himself. Every incident of his life, joy or sadness, was brought in prayer to God with a childlike, trusting faith and a willingness to accept His will for every step on what often proved to be a prickly path.

Only toward himself was he merciless; and sometimes his self-condemnation seemed to be outside the bounds of common sense.

On July twelfth Lydia's letter arrived with the first mail from England. It told Henry she thought of him in prayer every day and the whole letter sounded full of promises to his lovesick heart, rousing the old longings. His peace of mind was disturbed and he began to wonder if, after all, it could be God's will for them to marry.

The thought persisted and eventually Henry discussed the whole matter with David Brown, asking him to read the letter.

The older man was convinced that the lady was waiting to be won over, and he advised Henry to send a suitable reply.

Later that evening a lonely figure sat in his pagoda, his mind in a whirl, writing a courteously restrained love letter, with a definite proposal that his lady should come out to him as soon as possible. So sure was he now that Lydia would one day be with him in India that he asked if she could be ready to sail in the February fleet. In reality, it was actually well into March before she even received his letter.

The sun was rising in the dawn sky before Henry put down his pen, and in his heart rang the sound of wedding bells.

From then on he began to prepare for Lydia's arrival, brightening up his spartan home as much as possible. Among other things, he sent an order to Josiah Wedgwood, Queen Charlotte's potter as he was called, for a set of his latest "Queensware" cups and saucers being produced in the English county of Staffordshire.

Henry talked over plans with David Brown and his wife and it was arranged that Lydia should come initially as their guest. Mrs. Brown would go down to Calcutta to meet her and would then take her to Aldeen to stay until the marriage could be arranged.

Everything seemed to be slipping into place and the optimistic Henry was as excited as a schoolboy!

Chapter 15

NEW APPOINTMENTS

On September 13, 1806, Henry received his appointment to Dinapore, the European suburb of Patna, which was then the fifth largest city in India, stretching for some fourteen miles along the Ganges. Patna itself was predominantly Muslim. In the army settlement there were four hundred troops under the command of General Clarke.

Having become accustomed to the pleasant way of life at Aldeen, Henry now had to readjust to the more arduous and lonely life of a chaplain. But it also meant he would be fulfilling his great desire to get among the people of India and tell them of Jesus and his love. "I think that when my mouth is opened I shall preach to them day and night. I feel that they are my brethren in the flesh."

The Serampore missionaries, along with

other friends, joined the Brown family for a farewell meeting in Henry's garden pagoda, and on October fifteenth he had to say goodbye to them all. Henry was comforted by the verse David Brown had quoted from the first chapter of the book of Joshua: "Have not I sent you?" But it was with mixed feelings he boarded the budgerow waiting to take him along the river to Dinapore.

Now for the first time, he was alone with the native people, and on a trip that would last many weeks, calling at local places on the way. Progress was slow as they glided over the water, giving Henry the opportunity to enjoy the passing scenery along the river bank and to watch the rare birds that flew overhead. Here and there they saw white-washed temples with broad steps leading down to the water's edge.

Although the sun was merciless during the day, the mornings and evenings were chilly; at sunset when the budgerow was moored, the boatmen lit their supper fire and settled around it. Many were the tales they told as they sat smoking their hookahs before bedding down for the night.

Traffic on the river came to a standstill and boats were moored along the bank. In the eerie stillness the cry of a distant jackal would break into the soporific sound of water lapping against the sides of the vessel. Then the lonely traveler's thoughts would go to his well-loved sister in

Cornwall and his friends at Cambridge, and with a clutch at his heart he longed for that expected reply from Lydia.

During the day he studied with his native language secretary (moonshee); on October twentieth he recorded the fact that he had started translating the book of Acts into Hindustani (Urdu), writing it out in Persian characters. Henry realized that the best method of acquiring a knowledge of the various oriental tongues was to study Sanskrit; however, he found it difficult to conquer the grammar and wrote, "I cannot say where I am in it, being enveloped at present in a thick cloud with the exceptions, limitations, anomalies, etc."

Henry also records that later that day he shot a bird which he handed over to the cook, looking forward to a meal that would be a change from curry!

He went on shore often to meet the local people and found little difficulty getting into conversation with them. His sensitive ear was quick to notice the change of dialect as he passed from village to village. He also went into the markets on the river bank to distribute copies of the New Testament to those who said they could read. In this way, watching and listening, Henry learned more and more of the beliefs and traditions of the country he had adopted as his own.

On October twenty-seventh they moored at Berhampore and Henry went ashore to visit an army hospital, ministering to the European soldiers who were patients. When he met the surgeon he was surprised to find him to be an old school-fellow from Truro; Henry invited him back to the boat to spend the evening, giving them both the chance to talk of days gone by.

Another day he visited a village school at Mirdypore. "The little boys, seated cross-legged on the ground all round the room, read some of the New Testament to us. While the boys displayed their skills in reading their fathers and mothers crowded in great numbers round the doors." Proud parents—the same the world over!

And so at last, after six interesting weeks, the chaplain came to his new parish, moving into barrack quarters on November 26, 1806. There was no welcome for him and there had been little preparation for his coming. His duties were to include taking services, but he found no church. Thus services had to be conducted either in a barrack room with no seating or in one of the squares which provided no shade from the hot sun. It was little wonder the soldiers were apathetic in their response.

Henry also tried to introduce church services at Bankipore, the civilian settlement, but here again he was discouraged by the attitude of his own countrymen. The people seemed to resent his presence among them—particularly his friendly approach to the natives.

He continued with translation, working on the Parables and the Book of Common Prayer. By June 1807 he could write, "In Hindustani translation I begin to feel my ground and can go on much faster than one moonshee can follow." Increasingly he was aware that his gift as a linguist exceeded his suitability as a chaplain. His evangelistic sermons were not popular and seemed to make very little impression on most of his congregation. They wanted their religion to be a little less severe!

Henry was, however, kept busy with army matters and fulfilled his duties with sincerity and compassion. There were often funerals to conduct. There were also sick men in the hospital to visit—and to these he brought cheer and comfort.

On one occasion, Henry had to travel seventy danger-ridden miles in an uncomfortable covered litter (palanquin) in order to preside at the wedding of two of his parishioners. Before setting off, he left work for his moonshee to get on with in his absence and prudently made out his will!

His friends, Brown and Corrie, wrote to him regularly and their letters were to Henry as refreshing as snow in summer heat; their support was invaluable to this solitary worker. Major and Mrs. Young, who invited Henry often to a meal in their home, were the only friends near at hand.

Henry had a flair for mingling with the

"man in the street"; learning as he talked with them, finding out more of the prejudices, aspirations, and attitudes of Asian people. His scholarly mind delighted in discussion, especially when the subject was that of the varying forms of worship and religion. After listening courteously to the opinion of others he would lead his hearers back to the truths found in the Scriptures. "My thirst for knowledge is very strong but I pray continually that the Spirit of God may hold the reins."

When the hot, dry winds that scorch the upland plains made barrack quarters unbearable, Henry was allocated a spacious bungalow in one of the "cantonment" squares. He immediately put aside the large central room and verandahs for a church and kept only the smaller rooms for his personal use. He put in benches to seat the congregation and a table behind which he stood to take the services, while the army band led the singing.

It was encouraging that there was now a small group of soldiers who came to his room during the week for Bible study and prayer. Sometimes he spread out a "fair white linen cloth" and held a Communion service for them.

There were many Indian and Portuguese women who had become an institution in camp life, and for these there was no shepherd. Though nominally Catholic or Muslim they understood little of any faith, and Henry was concerned for their spiritual welfare. He arranged to have a special service in the native tongue and asked the Sergeant-Major to give public notice of the fact. The result was that about two hundred women turned up for the first service. Regrettably, he could never be sure how much they understood of his faltering Urdu.

His next concern was for the native urchins that haunted the bazaars, learning nothing but the ways of the world. Henry set up primary schools; and for the pupils who learned to read, he prepared in Urdu some of the Bible stories as their textbook.

During the year, he was distressed to hear from Cornwall that his older sister, Laura, had died from tuberculosis, and that Sally too was far from well. The news emphasized and multiplied the many thousand miles that separated him from his family. His own health was also causing him concern.

But there was sunshine among the clouds, for although the transfer of Major and Mrs. Young to another district had left Henry feeling destitute of close friends, there were to be others to take their place: Paymaster Sherwood of the 53rd Regiment was on his way to Cawnpore with his wife. When they reached Dinapore they decided to leave their budgerow (keelless barge) and call on Henry, who invited them to stay at his bungalow for the night.

Mrs. Sherwood was a writer, and with skill she recorded her impressions of people and places. Her book *The Life of Mrs. Sherwood* includes her description of the first meeting with Henry Martyn and gives a much more realistic picture of the man than can be deduced from his journal:

"He was dressed in white and looked very pale, which however was nothing singular in India. His hair, a light brown, was raised from his forehead, which was a remarkably fine one. His features were not regular but his expression was so luminous, so intellectual, so affectionate, so beaming with Divine charity that no one could have looked at his features and thought of their shape or form—instead the out-beaming of his soul would absorb the attention of every observer. There was a very decided air, too, of the gentleman about Mr. Martyn and a perfection of manners which, from his extreme attention to all minute civilities, might seem almost inconsistent with the general bent of his thoughts to the most serious subjects. He was as remarkable for ease as for cheerfulness, and in these particulars his journal does not give a graphic account. . . .

"After breakfast Mr. Martyn had family prayers which he commenced by singing a hymn. He had a rich deep voice and a fine taste for vocal music. After singing he read a chapter, explained parts of it and prayed extempore. Afterwards he withdrew to his studies."

She described him as "walking in this turbulent world with peace in his mind and charity in his heart."

Unfortunately, that peace of mind was once again to be shattered, and Henry desperately needed what Mrs. Sherwood called "charity in his heart."

On October 24, 1807, the longed-for reply of Lydia came from Cornwall. To Henry's dismay he read that Lydia was not coming out to him in India. It was a long, obscure letter, giving as her only reason the fact that her mother would not give her consent.

As a mature adult Lydia did not need this before taking any action, and here again her behavior is difficult to understand. Was Lydia's response a strict adherence to parental authority or an excuse to cover up doubts in her mind? Did she love Henry enough, aside from her mother's opinion, to follow him to the ends of the earth? No one can say.

Henry was thrown back on his faith as he attempted to conquer his grief and disappointment. In his answer to the letter he wrote, "I shall have to groan long perhaps, with a heavy heart; but if I am not hindered materially by it in the work of God, it will be for the benefit of my soul. . . ."

But when he wrote to David Brown with the news, his words showed more of the heartache that he hid from others. "It is as

I feared. She refuses to come because her mother will not give her consent. Sir, you must not wonder at my pale looks when I receive so many hard blows on my heart. . . . The Queensware on its way out to me can be sold at an outcry [auction] or given to Corrie. I do not want Queensware or anything else." This decree was not a petulant outburst but more a sigh of resignment.

Even as Henry was suffering the loss of so much of the world's joys and compensations, his devotion to Christ remained as strong as ever—the guiding principle in every part of his life.

CHAPTER 16

TRANSLATION AND SABAT

There had been a request from the Baptist missionaries in Calcutta for Henry to translate the New Testament into Urdu, and also into Arabic and Persian. David Brown wrote that they were sending an assistant to help with translation work. This was Sabat; an Arab who had become a Christian and wanted to serve the God he now worshiped.

In due time Sabat arrived and brought with him not only his wife but his wild, prickly nature that had not yet been wholly refined by grace! Again it is the writing of Mrs. Sherwood in her autobiography that gives a vivid picture of this "son of the desert":

"Every feature in the large disc of Sabat's face was what we should call exaggerated.

His eyebrows were arched, black, and strongly penciled; his eyes were dark and round and from time to time flashing with unsubdued emotion, and ready to kindle to flame on the most trifling occasion. His nose was high, his mouth wide, and his teeth large, looking white in contrast with his bronzed complexion and fierce black mustachio. He was a large and powerful man, and generally wore a skullcap of rich shawling or embroidered silk. . . . This son of the desert never sat in a chair without contriving to tuck up his legs under him on the seat. . . . The only languages which he was able to speak were Persian, Arabic, and a very little bad Hindustani; but what was wanting in the words of this man was more than made up by the loudness with which he uttered them, for he had a voice like roaring thunder.

"He would often contend for a whole morning about the meaning of an unimportant word; and Mr. Martyn has not unseldom ordered his palanquin and come over to us, to get out of the sound of the voice of the fierce Ishmaelite."

As was to be expected, Sabat proved both a joy and a trial to Henry; many were the storms encountered, as recorded in Henry's journal. When one of the servants offended the giant he vowed revenge, trembling with uncontrolled rage until finally soothed by the patient, understanding chaplain; then "the wild beast fell asleep!"

Sabat was provided with a bungalow but worked and ate with Henry. At first neither approved of the plans and ideas of the other; but his master persevered with this new firebrand, and in their own way each influenced and helped the other.

Sometimes the proud Arab was tearfully remorseful and confessed his failure in the Christian life: "Why am I like this after believing for three years? Every day I determine to keep Christ crucified in my sight, but I forget to think of him. I rejoice when I remember God's love in Christ, but I am like a sheep—feeding happily while he looks at the grass, but when he looks behind and sees the lion he can't eat."

His faithful friend assured him that all Christians experience a disappointment in themselves; but like Paul the apostle, they learn gradually that with Christ at the helm they will be able to say, "I can do all things through Christ who strengthens me" (Philippians 4:13).

Sabat was also jealous of Mirza, the Muslim who arrived shortly after him to help with the Urdu translation of the New Testament. He spoke of Mirza only with contempt. He was angry that Henry did not hate him too, quoting the Arabic proverb that a friend is the enemy of a friend's enemy.

But Henry liked Mirza and found him invaluable in the work they were doing together—although the continual conflict between his two helpers caused him distress. At last, in spite of Henry's appeals to stay until the translation was finished, Mirza found it impossible to put up with Sabat any longer and resigned before the four Gospels were completed.

In the meantime, Henry's health was steadily deteriorating and in January 1808 he wrote, "I found pains in my chest for the first time, a consequence of over-speaking." At the end of the day he would be breathless and completely exhausted. "I had better take warning in time, before I am put on the shelf." He suffered an attack of fever in September and had to cancel engagements "because of the weak and sore state of my lungs." As he sought to regain strength he had a great longing to feel again the bracing air of his native land instead of the humid atmosphere of the Indian rainy season.

Then in April 1809 Henry heard from the military authorities that he was being transferred to Cawnpore, three hundred miles farther up the river. Even for someone in good health, it would have been a daunting journey to contemplate in the hottest part of the year; but, leaving Sabat to do the packing with instructions to follow later, Henry set off in a palanquin to tackle the many wearisome miles on land.

It was indeed a foolish mistake for Henry to attempt such a journey at the hottest and worst period of the year. He could have asked for permission to postpone it to a more suitable month; or he could have arranged to go to Cawnpore in a budgerow along the river. Instead he suffered the discomfort of the palanquin—deciding to travel only at night when the hot winds, which blew like a furnace fire, would be less severe.

On reaching Allahabad he found there was no stopping place between there and Cawnpore; this meant continuing the journey for two days and nights without a pause. The uncomfortable palanquin could do nothing to keep out the fierceness of the hot winds, as the four bearers jerked it along the dusty path.

It was a mercy that Henry's friends, the Sherwoods, who had stayed with him at Dinapore on their way to Cawnpore, were now installed there with the 53rd Regiment. On May third the Sherwoods were about their various tasks; the paymaster was at a table with his account books while behind grass screens under the cloth fan (punkah) the pregnant Mrs. Sherwood lay on her couch resting.

On a diminutive chair at her side sat Annie, the little orphan girl rescued and adopted by the Sherwoods. As the child played, the long, black plait hanging down her back looked strangely heavy against her small, contented face. Near her was a small green box complete with precious lock and key, and in this were stored her few treasures.

Quiet as a little happy mouse she dressed her doll or looked up verses in her Bible, marking the place carefully with minute pieces of paper.

It was too hot for much conversation and only the click of the punkah or the wail of the hot wind outside broke the silence. Suddenly there came the sound of footsteps and Mr. Sherwood went to the side of the house to investigate. His wife heard him exclaim "Mr. Martyn!" and a moment later he led in the exhausted chaplain, who collapsed on the floor.

The lethargy of the household disappeared in a frantic preparation to find the coolest place to put up the obviously ill traveler, and a couch was brought into the central hall. There Henry lay for many days, too ill to lift his head from the pillow. The heat of the journey remained in his blood and the motion of the palanquin stayed in his brain to torment him. Much later he wrote to David Brown, "I transported myself with such rapidity to this place that I nearly transported myself out of the world."

When the hot winds subsided they left a stifling stillness which was even more unbearable for the invalid; but Mrs. Sherwood cared lovingly for him, treating him as one of her household. As he recovered strength his old cheeriness returned, and with his precious books around him his convalescence in this home proved to be a happy contentment.

The child, Annie, her large eyes gazing sympathetically at the man who had lain day after day on the couch, gradually overcame her shyness. She would often bring her chair and her green box to sit quietly beside him. He asked to see her treasures and she showed him also the Bible verses she had marked. It was not long before they were the best of friends.

This highly qualified man, who in his Cambridge days had won the mathematics honor of being Senior Wrangler, found it easy to interest himself in the thoughts of an Asian child. He enjoyed her daily visits, which did their share in his healing.

Though Mrs. Sherwood mothered him, she did not fully understand some of the religious views nor the naivety of her lovable invalid. She scolded him when she found out he had sent off one of the coolies to withdraw the salary which had accumulated during Henry's illness.

"What?" she said, "With so large a sum there would be a temptation to any coolie to make off with it." The man returned safely with the money, but it was only the trusting Henry who expressed no surprise!

When he was well enough he went to look around his new station and prepare to again take up his chaplain's duties. His first impression of Cawnpore was a disappointment. There was no church for services, and "not so much as the fly of a tent"; and all he could do about it was to apply to Lord Minto, the Governor General, to requisition a building.

Eventually the authorities were willing for one of the existing bungalows to be adapted for church services. But the first service, on May fourteenth, had to be conducted out of doors on the parade ground. It was excessively hot and some of the soldiers dropped where they stood beneath the burning rays of the sun. It was amazing that Henry, who was still a convalescent, somehow received strength to carry on.

When the rains came, all outdoor parades were cancelled and services were held in a riding school, where the lingering smell of horses could hardly produce an atmosphere of worship.

Henry bought two houses near one another; one for himself, and a smaller one for Sabat and his wife, when they finally arrived with the furniture and goods from Dinapore.

Sabat settled down to work with a will, helping with the translation into Arabic and Persian. "He is gentle and almost as diligent as I could wish. Everything seems to please him. His bungalow joins mine and is very neat. So from morning to night we work together and the work goes forward. The first two or three days he translated into Arabic and I was his scribe; but this being too fatiguing to me, we have been since that at the Persian."

Unfortunately, when the novelty of his new home wore off Sabat lapsed into apathy, eager to find any excuse to shut up books for the day, being satisfied to get through just one chapter.

Henry was also concerned about the quality of Sabat's Persian, but any criticism only made Sabat angry. "I did not come from Persia to India to learn Persian."

Henry heard from Mirza that he was willing to come back provided Sabat was not around. Although this meant constant vigilance on the part of the harassed peacekeeper, he felt it worthwhile to secure once again the help of this valuable language teacher. Revision of the Urdu New Testament was begun in earnest.

At this time Henry discovered an increasing fascination for Hebrew, which he found to be a help in understanding other languages. He wrote to ask David Brown to send him grammars and dictionaries of all the languages of the earth. "Do not stare, Sir. I have no ambition to become a linguist; but they will help me in some inquiries I am making."

Not a linguist? The man was already a dedicated and gifted student of languages and was applying his genius to the translation of the New Testament into the three great tongues of the Near East.

Yet for all his thirst for knowledge and learning he also wrote, "I would rather have the smallest portion of love and humility than the knowledge of an arch-angel!"

To counteract the strains and stresses of his busy life Henry would often go at sunset to call on his friends. Mrs. Sherwood wrote, "Two or three times a week he used to come. He sat his horse as if he were not quite aware that he was on horseback, and he generally wore his coat as if it were falling from his shoulders!"

CHAPTER 17

DEATH OF SALLY

When he was at home, Henry's house was always full of people—with scribes copying translations surrounded by manuscripts and dictionaries, with soldiers who were keen enough to come for Bible study and prayer, and with beggars who knew where they would be given a handful of rice. To the latter he let it be known that his alms would be handed out only once a week; each Sunday his gates were thrown open to admit the motley crowd. It was the unpredictable Sabat who suggested that the chaplain ought to hold special services for them.

Accordingly, the following Sunday when some four hundred had gathered in his garden, Henry addressed them. He said he gave with pleasure what alms he could afford but wished to give them something better—the riches to be found in an understanding of God. This was the first of the services he was to hold for them—services which continued right up to the time of leaving Cawnpore. Throughout, it remained an exacting ordeal.

It was a congregation of mixtures, as Mrs. Sherwood recorded in her book. "They were young and old, male and female, tall and short, athletic and feeble, bloated and wizened; some clothed in abominable rags, some nearly without clothes; a temperature often rising above 92°F. while the sun poured its burning rays upon us through a lurid haze of dust. . . . I still imagine that I hear the calm, distinct and musical tones of Henry Martyn as he stood raised above the people."

They were a noisy lot, often interrupting the preacher with shouts and sneers and curses, and he needed to wait for the storm to pass before continuing. Each week he needed to seek courage, and when the service was over it would leave him in a state of collapse.

Henry often wondered whether he had been the means of doing the smallest good to any one of the strange people who, he believed, came chiefly for the coins he gave them when it was over. He never knew that on that first Sunday there had been a group of rich young men passing the end of his garden who were curious about the strange proceedings and stopped to listen.

One, a Muslim, a professor of Persian and Arabic, heard enough to want to learn more, though telling no one of his interest. He approached Sabat and became employed as copier of the Persian Gospels. One day he was given charge of a complete copy of the Persian New Testament to take to the bookbinder.

He retained it long enough to read it all before passing it on; and he believed what he read, eventually accepting the truths for himself. Records show that this man was baptized by David Brown in 1811 under the name of Abdel Musseeh, going on to become a clergyman and a notable Christian leader.

Letters from England sometimes included one from Lydia, who seemed to have a flair for prolonging emotional conflicts. Each time Henry saw her handwriting his heart beat a little faster; but her letters were only to emphasize her decision not to come to India and marry him.

Henry was deeply distressed to hear that his sister Sally was now suffering from the family complaint of tuberculosis. Within a few days he was given the news that she had died. Grief overwhelmed him. Sally was the dearest and the last of his family, and now he was completely alone. In despair the words of Elijah came to him: "I, even I only, am left" (1 Kings 19:14, RSV).

When writing to console him, Lydia suggested she might take the place of the sister he had lost. This began a new series of letters between them.

By April 1810 Henry's health was so bad he had to reduce his speaking engagements, finding little strength for his basic duties. He had to confess to his friends, Brown and Corrie, that his chest pains were becoming alarming, and Corrie was given leave to go to Cawnpore to help. He brought with him his sister Mary who had come out to India, and together they settled down to look after the invalid. Corrie took over the preaching, and Mary came each day from the Sherwood's house where she was staying, helping with domestic arrangements for Henry. This meant he was able to concentrate more fully on the translations without overtaxing his strength, and after four months his health improved.

With a "dog-in-the-manger" attitude Lydia must have written to Henry about Mary Corrie, for in a letter to her he says, "You thought it possible your letter might find me married, or about to be so. Let me begin with assuring you, with more truth than Gehazi did his master, 'Thy servant went not whither.' My heart has not strayed from Marazion or wherever you are."

By June there had been great progress with the Arabic New Testament. Although Henry wrote, "We shall never find in India so good a man as Sabat," he was concerned over the many inaccuracies that had to be corrected in the Arab's translation work.

For some time Henry's eyes had been turned toward Arabia and Persia, and his conversations with Sabat increased his desire to visit these countries for himself.

He realized that in the Arabic translation, Sabat's grammar needed more care, and that in the Persian, his writing was interspersed with faulty Arabic phrases. But it was impossible to convince the bombastic Arab of anything wrong with his work.

At last Henry wrote to David Brown suggesting that the only way to succeed with the translations would be to take the Arabic New Testament to Arabia for improvement, "having under the other arm the Persian to be examined at Shiraz. If my life is spared there is no reason why the Arabic should not be done in Arabia and the Persian in Persia, as well as the Indian in India."

There had been great satisfaction among the missionaries in Calcutta over the Urdu New Testament, and hope for the Arabic; but the Persian was found to have too many Arabic idioms in it for it to be realistic for the average reader. So Henry's suggestion began to take root; this might be the answer.

Plans for him to travel to Arabia and Persia (modern Iran) were put into operation, and the army General at Cawnpore was approached with an application for leave of absence for the chaplain. There was no hesitation in granting him unlimited sick-leave.

On Henry's last Sunday at Cawnpore the building he had worked for was complete, and the new bell rang to call his flock to the opening service. Corrie read the prayers, the regimental band played for the singing, and Henry preached his first and last sermon in the new church.

Before he left Cawnpore he decided to burn all his memoranda. Fortunately Corrie persuaded him not to do that, suggesting that all the papers should be packaged and sealed, and that he would keep them safe until Henry's return. Among other things the parcel contained Henry's precious journal, which was thus preserved safely.

CHAPTER 18

EN ROUTE FOR PERSIA

On October 1, 1810, Henry said goodbye to his kind friends at Cawnpore and boarded the budgerow to take him down the river to the base at Calcutta. On the way they called at Allahabad, Benares, and Patna to renew acquaintance; but for most of the month the chaplain was alone with his books and his exciting dreams for the future.

It was four years since he had left Calcutta, and to be on his way to Aldeen once more it was very much like going home. When he arrived, the Brown family gave him a royal welcome, "the children jumping, shouting, and convoying me in troops to the house. They are a lovely family and I don't know when I have felt so delighted as at family worship that night."

For the next ten weeks he spent his time between Aldeen and the missionaries at

Serampore, while he prepared for the journey to Arabia and Persia.

It was an added joy to meet an old friend from Cambridge, Thomas Thomasson, who had been Simeon's senior curate before following Henry to India to give the rest of his life to that country's service. Thomasson was now living in the heart of Calcutta with his wife and family, gathering a home together.

Both the Browns and Thomasson were shocked at the change in their friend. "He is much altered, is thin and sallow, but he has the same loving heart." Knowing that Simeon was anxious to have the latest news of Henry's health, Thomasson wrote to tell him, "He is on his way to Arabia where he is going in pursuit of health and knowledge. You know his genius and what gigantic strides he takes in everything. He has some great plan in his mind of which I am no competent judge, but as far as I understand it, the object is far too grand for one short life, and much beyond his feeble and exhausted frame. . . . But let us hope that the sea air may revive him. In all other respects he is exactly the same as he was; he shines in all the dignity of love; and seems to carry about him such a heavenly majesty as impresses the mind beyond description. . . ."

During this time of waiting at Calcutta Henry was able to fulfil a five-year-old promise to Simeon to have his portrait painted. When completed this was sent home to India House to be collected. It was a "striking likeness"; but when Simeon saw it he was distressed to see the change in his former curate. "I couldn't bear to look up on it but turned away . . . covering my face."

In Calcutta there was nothing but praise for the Urdu New Testament, but again it was stressed that Sabat's Persian needed polishing. Thus Henry determined to go first to Persia, and after that perhaps to Damascus or Baghdad and into the heart of Arabia.

He had an interview with Lord Minto, the Governor General of India. Minto listened sympathetically to the enthusiastic, pale young man with the wide vision—and granted him leave to proceed with his fantastic plans.

Armenian friends in Calcutta wrote an introduction for him to take to their relatives in Persia, commending Henry to their fellowship and care. "I now pass from India to Arabia, not knowing the things that shall befall me there, but assured that an ever-faithful God and Saviour will be with me in all places wherever I go. May He guide and protect me and after prospering me in the thing unto which I go, bring me back again to my delightful work in India."

But it was not easy to find a ship willing to take aboard this disturbing clergyman, whose evangelical zeal was now well known. One captain refused to have him on board in case he tried to convert the Arab sailors, lest this should cause a mutiny! At last Henry managed to secure a passage on a boat going to Bombay by way of Ceylon and Goa. This boat was taking Mountstuart Elphinstone, former ambassador in Kabul, to his post as the new British Resident at Poona.

They were to sail on January 7, 1811. Henry could not bring himself to say goodbye to his Calcutta friends, so he slipped quietly away. "Leaving Calcutta was so much like leaving England that I went on board my boat without giving them notice."

For the whole of the six weeks before they reached Bombay, Henry enjoyed thoroughly the companionship of the kindly man who was to become the Governor of Bombay. Elphinstone had a wide knowledge of India and the two men stimulated each other as they discussed many intellectual subjects.

This important man seems to have been impressed with his fellow-traveler and wrote to a friend: "We have in Mr. Martyn an excellent scholar and one of the mildest, most cheerful, and most pleasant men I ever saw."

The letter continues, "He is extremely religious and disputes with the Abyssinian about the faith, but he talks on all subjects and makes others laugh as heartily as he could do if he were an infidel! . . . His zeal is not troublesome; he does not press disputes or investigate creeds. He is a man of good sense and taste, simple in his manners and character, and cheerful in his conversation."

When the boat called at Ceylon, the two men went on shore and walked to a cinnamon garden along a pleasant road beneath groves of coconut trees. Among the trees were native tents, and beyond them there were glimpses of the sea. Henry found time to procure a piece of the aromatic bark to send with his next letter to Lydia; at the same time he described to her the Indian coastline they passed as they went on to Bombay: "At a distance green waves seem to wash the foot of the mountain, but on a nearer approach little churches were seen. . . . Was it this maritime situation that recalled to my mind Perran Church . . . or made my thoughts wander on the beach to the east of Lamorran? You don't tell me whether you ever walk there and imagine the billows that break at your feet to have made their way from India." Poor Henry! He kept searching the clouds for any break in them that would bring him comfort in his relationship with Lydia.

At Goa he visited the tomb of St. Francis Xavier; but he lost interest in the Italian paintings and bronze figures when the friar who was showing him around mentioned something about "the grace of God in the heart." Within minutes Henry was deep in earnest conversation with the friar!

When they reached Bombay he became a guest at Government House for five weeks and, thanks to his friendship with Elphinstone, was introduced to other important people there. These introductions included Sir James Mackintosh, Recorder of Bombay, who later wrote in his journal, "Elphinstone introduced me to a young clergyman called Martyn. He seems to be a mild and benevolent enthusiast. . . . Martyn the saint dined here. We had the novelty of grace before and after dinner, all the company standing. We later had two or three hours good discussion on grammar and metaphysics."

Henry was also introduced to Sir John Malcolm, a soldier and diplomat who had twice been sent to Persia to establish British trade and prestige in that country. At present he was in Bombay writing a history of Persia, and he was generous with his information. This was a valuable contact—someone with whom Henry could talk of Persia and her political and commercial aspects.

Sir John Malcolm gave Henry letters of introduction to important people he would be likely to meet in Bushire, Shiraz, and Isfahan in Persia. He also wrote to Sir Gore Ouseley, British Ambassador in Persia.

"I warned Martyn not to move from Bushire without your sanction. His intention is to go via Shiraz and Isfahan to Baghdad in an attempt to discover ancient copies of the Gospels, which he and others are persuaded lie hidden in the mountains of Persia. His knowledge of Arabic is superior to that of any Englishman in India. He is altogether a very learned and cheerful man, but a great enthusiast in his holy calling. . . . I told him I thought you would require him to act with great caution and not allow his zeal to run away with him. . . . His good sense and great learning will delight you, while his constant cheerfulness will add to the hilarity of your party."

It is of course possible that Henry had told Malcolm of a desire to include in his itinerary a search for old manuscripts; however, this is not recorded in his journal. Perhaps Sir John had misunderstood. It is certain that Henry's main interest in going to Persia was to live among the people, learn all he could of their customs and culture, and improve his knowledge of their language—all while translating the New Testament into perfect Persian.

While in Bombay he was, as usual, on the lookout for an opportunity to mingle with the local people. "I am visited from morning till night by the learned natives who are drawn here by the Arabic tract I composed to help Sabat, but which the scribe I employed has been showing around."

He had many long discussions with his

visitors, especially with a Parsee poet named Feeroz who spoke Persian and was familiar with Arabic. "He is considered the most learned man here . . . and possesses one of the most agreeable qualities a disputant can possess, which is patience. He never interrupted me; and if I rudely interrupted him, he was silent in a moment." Henry's gentlemanly nature appreciated courtesy in others.

Feeroz was not impressed with the New Testament translations Henry showed him—though he was amused by some of the Arabic words. His criticism was helpful as it pointed out mistakes in Sabat's Persian.

When Henry told him the translator was an Arab who had lived in Persia, Feeroz replied crisply, "An Arab, if he lives there twenty years, will never speak Persian well."

One day the caller was a very young man, son of Lord Wellesley's Envoy to Persia. At first Henry thought he seemed such a boy that there would not be much point in arguing with him; however, when the visitor spoke it was obvious he had a powerful command of the Persian language. This was a delight to Henry. The young man was found to be familiar with all the arguments put forward by the Muslim scholars (mullahs), and the discussion proved helpful and interesting. "I thought that perhaps his youthful mind might be more open to conviction than that of the hoary mullahs."

Henry's conversation and discussions with so many people added fuel to the fire burning within him, intensifying his desire to get to Persia itself and proceed with further translation. He planned to get to Shiraz, the city of poets and learning—the center of Persia's culture. Here he expected to find the facilities he needed for his study of all things Persian, taking with him the various letters of introduction he had been given.

With as much patience as he could muster, he explored the best way to bring this about as quickly as possible.

CHAPTER 19

IN ORIENTAL DRESS

In the month of March, 1811, Henry was given a passage in an East India Company's ship *Benares* which was to cruise in the Persian Gulf, looking for Arab pirates. There were Europeans on board to whom he could act as chaplain, but they were in no way demanding of his services. Thus he had much time to himself for his continued language study.

"Every day I Hebraize. I resolve to read Arabic or Persian but before I am aware of it I am thinking about Hebrew. I have translated Psalm 16." He thought of sending the translation to his friend Thomasson in Calcutta, but wanted first to make sure that each part of it was correct. Had his friend and counselor been near at hand it is possible he would have advised the insatiable linguist to stay in the New Testament, where his translation gift was seen at its excellent best.

Apart from an initial bout of seasickness the voyage was a pleasant trip, the suspected pirates keeping well out of the way. "You will be happy to know that the murderous pirates against whom we were sent, having received notice of our approach, are all got out of the way. So, I am no longer liable to be shot in a battle, or to decapitation after!"

On April twenty-first the *Benares* anchored at Muscat. There it lay for a week in a small cove surrounded by rocks, which held the heat and kept out the air. Shore leave was not encouraged as the area around Muscat was unsafe. Instead of taking this advice, Henry went with Captain Lockett to see some of the sights and to walk through the fascinating bazaars, accompanied by an Arab soldier and his African servant. The African boy was so keenly interested in talking about Muhammad and Christianity that the following day Henry gave him a copy of the Gospels in Arabic. Though it may have been only the joy of possession that gave the boy so much delight, he took it away as a great prize to be treasured—and, as Henry fervently hoped, to be read.

After leaving Muscat, the ship had a rough passage for some days in the great funnel of the Gulf; but before they reached Bushire Henry wrote in his journal: "May 7: I finished a work on which I have been engaged for a fortnight: a new arrangement of all the Hebrew roots, classing them according to the last letter, the last but one, and so on."

On May twenty-second they landed, and Henry set foot for the first time on Persian soil—another step toward the fulfilment of his translation plans. He was determined, God willing, not to leave Persia until he had in his hand a New Testament translation that would satisfy the most fastidious Persian.

Henry always felt that the best way to get to know the people of a foreign land was to look as much like them as possible; so to travel into the interior, Henry decided to wear Persian dress.

While this was being made for him he set about discovering Persian and Arabic reactions to his first translations. One day he called on the Governor, a Persian Khan; "He was so particular in his attentions, seating me in his own seat and then sitting by my side. After the usual salutations and inquiries the hookah [smoking-pipe] was introduced; then coffee in china cups placed within silver ones; then hookah; then some rose-water syrup; then hookah. As there were often long intervals in which naught was heard but the gurgling of the hookah, I looked round with some anxiety for something to discourse upon. Observing the windows to be of stained glass, I began to question him about the art of coloring glass. . . ."

Another day a well-known Turk came to visit Henry. "He is a great Arabic scholar and came to see how much we knew; or rather, if the truth were known, to show how much he himself knew!"

By May thirtieth the Persian costume was ready, and it was time to start the journey to Shiraz. Friends back at Calcutta might have had difficulty in recognizing this man. He was still writing his journal, and before starting for Shiraz he recorded: "The Persian dress consists of, first, stockings and shoes in one; next, a pair of large blue trousers or else a pair of huge red boots; then, the shirt; then, the tunic; and above it, the coat and a great-coat, both of chintz. I have here described my own dress, most of which I have on at this moment. On the head is worn an enormous cone with wool on it, made of the skin of the black Tartar sheep. If to this description of my dress I add that my beard and mustache have been suffered to vegetate undisturbed ever since I left India, that I am sitting on a Persian carpet in a room without tables or chairs, and that I bury my hand in the dish without waiting for spoon or plate, you will give me credit for being already an accomplished Oriental!"

Henry's new servant, Zechariah, an Armenian from Isfahan, livened the preparations with his cheerful chatter. He had the gift of being able to find something to say to anyone who would listen!

Most of the company traveled on mules but some rode horseback. The muleteer offered Henry his own horse, complete with the bell fastened round its neck. One of the travelers, a Bombay trumpeter, was on his way to join the Embassy at Shiraz and he was asked to announce the departure with a blow on his instrument. He might have been a learner or perhaps his trumpet was out of order, but the frightful sounds that emerged did nothing but startle the animals and cause amusement to the humans!

There followed a deal of jostling, arguing and restraining of recalcitrant mules before each one found his place, and in an orderly fashion the cavalcade moved out through the gates of the city.

It was nearing midnight, the fine moonlit night punctuated by the sound of tinkling bells and the tramp of hooves over the hard, rocky ground of the Oriental scene. As night advanced the noisy party grew quiet, and one of the muleteers began to softly sing a sad, plaintive song.

By sunrise they had completed about twenty miles and pitched tent under a tree. The heat became intense, rising to an unbearable 112°F. Henry wrapped himself in a blanket in an attempt to keep out the burning heat and keep in the moisture of his body.

When the fierce sun went down, plans had to be made to proceed; and while the mules were being loaded up Henry was able at last to get an hour's sleep, waking refreshed in the cool night air. Henry's ebullient Armenian servant was here, there, and everywhere, talking incessantly and seeking to encourage the party by word and gesture.

At the next calling place the travelers quickly made a "tatty," or matting of cuscus grass, with the branches of a date tree. They then employed a peasant to keep it well watered. By this means they were able to keep the temperature through the day below 114°F. Even so Henry needed to wrap a wet towel round his head and body. A neighboring village was able to supply them with milk and food for their meal.

During the night they reached the foot of the mountains, but instead of the clearer air they expected they were greeted by the suffocating smell of naptha. "We saw a river, but what flowed in it seemed difficult to say—whether it were water or green oil. It scarcely moved, and the stones which it laved it left of a greyish color—as if its foul touch had given them the leprosy." An unpleasant experience, crowned by the fact that Zechariah fell from his mule and was rather bruised, putting a damper on the whole company. "He looked very sorrowful and had lost much of his garrulity!"

The next morning the cavalcade found a grove of date trees and decided to camp, hoping for shade through the day; instead, the atmosphere at sunrise proved far hotter in the grove than the surrounding areas. So that evening they welcomed the cooler, clear air as they began to ascend the mountains, although the going was more difficult. As they wound their way round the narrow paths on the high rocks over-looking deep and dangerous precipices, they had to be alert every moment. Here a false step could prove fatal and send them hurtling down the mountainside.

The animals they had to depend on were used to the terrain and fortunately their step was sure—there was no room for mistakes. "There was nothing to mark the road but the rocks being a little more worn in one place than another. Sometimes my horse stopped as though to consider about the way. For myself I couldn't guess where the road lay; but he always found it."

The scenery was grand and impressive and Henry would have been the first to appreciate its grandeur; but the extra fatigue he felt through lack of sleep made him insensitive to all around him. Only his invincible spirit and determination to fulfill the task ahead carried him along.

They were able to ride briskly when they came to the mountain plain, still finding it necessary to travel in the night and try to get what sleep they could during the heat of the day.

They slowly descended into a fertile valley where they saw fields of wheat and barley growing. An occasional tree would remind Henry of an autumn morning in England, with the temperature a blissful 62°F. Another scene was a green valley near a stream where clover grew in abundance; here cattle browsed in the adjoining fields. With a thankful heart Henry wrote in his journal, "He makes me to lie down in green pastures and leads me beside still waters" (Psalm 23).

This was a journey full of contrasts. At one point, when the temperature registered 110°F., the cavalcade met a mountaineer traveling down to Bushire with a load of ice. At that moment his load was to the hot and thirsty travelers more precious than gold, and they persuaded him to sell it to them.

The next night they climbed to a plain where the piercing wind cut like a knife and everyone was obliged to pile on all the clothes he could muster. Still they shivered!

CHAPTER 20

ROSES AND NIGHTINGALES

On June 9, 1811, the travelers came in sight of the orchards and gardens of Shiraz. The sun had set and the gates were already closed, but all around was the scent of herbs and roses, and the sound of nightingales.

Thankful that the nine days' trying journey—which today would take but a few hours—was over, Henry and his party camped for the night in a garden outside the walls.

The next day he rode in through the gates as soon as they were open—along the cypress-lined avenues of the city, past the elaborate mosques and the superbly tended gardens where Hafiz and other Persian poets lie buried. He caught sight of maidens, shyly peering out of the folds of their veils at the strange rider in his Persian dress; and gradually he reached the house of Jaffir Ali Khan. This was the leading citizen of high rank, to whom Henry carried his letter of introduction from Sir John Malcolm in Bombay.

It was refreshing beyond measure to arrive at this rich man's home and be graciously welcomed by Jaffir Ali, who immediately called for food for his visitors.

"After the long and tedious ceremony of coffee and pipes, breakfast made its appearance on two large trays. Curry, pilau, and various sweets cooled with snow and perfumed with rose-water were served in great profusion on china plates and dishes. There were a few wooden spoons beautifully carved—but being in Persian dress, and on the ground, I thought it high time to throw off the European, and so ate with my hands."

In his gracious manner Henry seemed always able to sense the "rightness" of things, and to adapt to the custom and culture of the company he was in—surely a valuable asset to any missionary!

Jaffir Ali made arrangements for a room in his large house to be set apart for his guest. Here Henry was able to unpack the books he had brought with him and ready for a concentrated attack on the Persian translation. This was to be his home for almost a year.

He found his host to be an understanding man of courteous manners, ever on the lookout for ways of adding to the comfort and pleasure of his guest.

As they talked, mostly on religious topics, it was obvious there was a complete absence of bigotry and prejudice. Jaffir Ali listened with an intellectual interest to Henry's plans for a perfect Persian translation of the New Testament. He later introduced his visitor to his brother-in-law, Seid Ali Khan, "who speaks the purest dialect of the Persian."

This new contact was interested in all Henry told him of his translation plans and offered to assist in making the new version. This offer proved to be a Godsend to the man who had come to Persia for the express purpose of "getting it right." Who better to help than one born in the country, who spoke "the purest dialect"? So, in little more than a week after arrival in Shiraz, Henry had started on the work he had come from India to do.

He found both Jaffir Ali and Seid Ali to be open-minded Sufis—the mystics of Islam—and their friendliness was helpful to one who knew what it was to be lonely in a crowd.

A stranger in a strange land, with only memories of all he had left to keep him company, Henry longed for Christian fellowship. He thought affectionately of Simeon in Cambridge, and Corrie and David Brown in India, remembering their many words of comfort and advice, and thanking

God afresh for them. Though separated by many miles, he was conscious that he still had their support.

It would seem that although he still had occasional bouts of fever and fatigue, Henry's health stabilized, if not improved, while he was at Shiraz.

Henry had written several letters to Lydia since leaving India, sending them by caravan to the coast or by Tartar courier to Constantinople, but there had been no reply. "Since ten months I have heard nothing of any one person whom I love. I read your letters incessantly and try to find something new, as I generally do. . . . I try to live on from day to day happy in His love and care."

So Lydia, truly loving but still rejecting him, flitted in and out of his life and thoughts—but never from the recesses of his heart.

CHAPTER 21

LIFE IN SHIRAZ

The British Ambassador, Sir Gore Ouseley, was in Shiraz for some weeks and Henry called on him, again with the letter of introduction from Sir John Malcolm. He was received kindly and was invited to preach to the household, after which he baptized their child.

As a stranger in the country Henry was anxious to pay due respect to the "powers that be." To this end, on July sixth he went to present himself to Prince Abbas Mirza, son of the Shah. "Early this morning I went with the Ambassador and his suite to court, wearing, agreeably to costume, a pair of red cloth stockings with green high-heeled shoes. When we entered the great court of the palace, a hundred fountains began to play. The Prince was at the opposite side in his talar (or hall of audience), seated on the ground. Here our first bow was made. When we came in sight of him we bowed a second time and entered the room. He did not rise, nor take notice of any but the Ambassador, with whom he conversed at the distance of the breadth of the room. . . ."

There was much local curiosity about the European who had taken up residence in the house of Jaffir Ali and mixed with the important people of the city. When he went shopping in the bazaar, carrying a list of his master's needs, the lively Zechariah was, for once, silent but "all ears." He made time to mingle with the crowds, alert to any mention of the lodger in the home of Jaffir Ali; and what he heard he was eager to pass on to the one concerned.

"Zechariah told me this morning that I was the town talk. It was asserted that I was come to Shiraz to be a Mussulman [Muslim], and should then bring five thousand men to Shiraz under pretence of making them Mussulmans, but in reality to take the city!"

In spite of his periodic eavesdropping, Zechariah attended well to his shopping and made sure the requirements of his master were properly met. The journal records, "Victuals are cheap . . . such a country for fruit I had no conception of. I have a fine horse which I bought for less than a hundred rupees, on which I ride every morning round the walls. My vain servant Zechariah, anxious that his master should appear like an ameer [ruler], furnished the horse with a saddle, or rather a pillion, which fairly covers his whole back. It has all the colors of the rainbow, but yellow is predominant; and from it hang down four large tassels also yellow."

The journal from this point becomes mostly a record of the progress of translation work and of Henry's discussions and disputes with the learned scholars of the city, to whom he reached out in friendship. He laid before them all that he believed to be true; but through it all ran the thread of his solitary witnessing to the faith of Jesus Christ.

Quickly he realized he would need to scrap the Persian copy of the Scriptures that he and Sabat had worked on in India. Without having his chaplain's duties to fulfil he would be able to give his whole time to translation, and with the help of Seid Ali he would start afresh and prepare a completely new version. Henry resolved to stay in Shiraz until this was finished. He wrote to tell Corrie in India of his decision, concluding the letter on a personal note:

"I go on as usual, riding round the walls in the morning and singing hymns at night over my milk and water—for tea I have none, though I want it! I am with you in spirit almost every evening and feel one with the saints of God all over the earth."

The greater part of the day was spent in his room working with Seid Ali, but they had to cope with many interruptions. Some callers came with a genuine desire to learn more of the Christian faith, seeking proof for the religion of Christ; others came only to argue, and some simply to scoff. But the grave and gentle stranger made himself available to all, ever ready to defend his faith.

One young scholar who on his first visit came to taunt found his attitude changing as he listened to the calm reasoning of this man of God—this man who knew that arguments are powerless until made effective by the Holy Spirit. Rahim returned many times until at last he was convinced of the truth. Before Henry left Shiraz he came again, this time to confess his belief. Later, when the Persian translation was finished, Henry gave Rahim one of the first copies which became his greatest treasure. One day he showed it to a Christian traveler he met, pointing to the words on the flyleaf. "There is joy in heaven over one sinner that repents." This was followed by the signature of Henry Martyn.

There were many Jews in Shiraz and, eager as always to learn, they were interested in the new teacher in the city. One of them who had become a Muslim came regularly to talk with Henry, asking him questions. "He showed himself extremely well read in the Hebrew Bible and the

Koran, quoting both with the utmost readiness. He said he must come every day and either make me a Mussulman or become himself a Christian."

So great was the general interest stirred up by the presence of the zealous Christian translator that the authorities became concerned. After deliberation they arranged for a treatise, *A Defense of Islam,* to be prepared by Mirza Ibrahim, who was known as the foremost of all the teachers. When this was presented to Henry with the idea of silencing him, he replied with a masterly series of tracts covering the whole controversy.

He was encouraged by the reaction of his helper, Seid Ali, to some of the passages of Scripture they were dealing with. "The poor boy, while reading how one of the servants of the High Priest struck the Lord on the face, stopped and said, 'Sir, did not his hand dry up?' "

Another day, while dealing with the twelfth chapter of John, Seid Ali exclaimed, "How he loved those twelve persons!" "Yes," replied Henry, "and all those who believe on Him through their word."

The two men often chatted together after the day's work was done. One evening Seid Ali confided the fact that ever since childhood he had been trying to find the truth in religion and was still undecided. Never before had he been given the opportunity of talking with those of another faith.

Gently Henry reminded him of the necessity of making up one's mind on such a subject, pointing him to the text they had recently been dealing with: "If any man's will is to do His will, he shall know whether the teaching is from God" (John 7:17, RSV).

Henry explained that this had been his own experience and when he could at last say before God, "What wilt Thou have me to do?" he had found peace.

During these talks Seid Ali was always reluctant to finish the conversation and one evening he said, with a smile, "You must not regret the loss of so much time as you give me, because it does me good."

Henry began to realize that his helper no longer argued about the truths they were translating together, as he had been inclined to do at first. His remarks now became more serious. One day when they were discussing the need to be humble in dealing with disputes in religion, Seid Ali confessed that he had no humility. "The truth is we are in a state of compound ignorance; ignorant, yet ignorant of our ignorance."

But Seid Ali was justly proud of what Henry and he had achieved in translation work, and when his friends called he would immediately produce the latest results, even though they ridiculed his enthusiasm. Then he would point out that, supposing he had received no other benefit, he had learned a lot. It was, he emphasized, much better to have gained so much knowledge about the Christian religion than to have frittered away the year idling in the gardens as they had done!

When July came Henry was given the opportunity to camp out. As a relief from the close confinement of life in a city house, his kind host had a tent pitched for him in one of the lovely gardens.

It was a tranquil spot beside a clear running stream, beneath the shade of an orange tree and surrounded by clusters of ripening grapes.

Here the two translators were able to work during the week with fewer interruptions; and here Henry could enjoy a quiet Sunday on his own. The lone worshipper wrote in his journal, "The first Sabbath morning I have had all to myself this long time, and I spent it with comfort and profit. I read Isaiah chiefly and hymns, which as usual brought to my remembrance the children of God in all parts of the earth."

CHAPTER 22

A BREAK FROM TRANSLATING

Although Henry's dedicated mind seemed closed to trivial matters, he was acutely aware of the beauty of creation, the wonders of science, and the history of past ages. During his stay at Shiraz he decided to set apart two days for a visit to the ancient city of Persepolis and see something of its fallen grandeur.

Persepolis, shrouded in mystery, unknown to the Greeks until the time of Alexander the Great, had once been the dynastic capital of Persia. It was here the many celebrations and festivals were held each year in the reign of Darius and Xerxes (about 400 BC). It was also the place chosen by Darius for his summer residence.

For the visit Henry arranged for two guards on horseback to accompany him and his servants, and when all was ready they started about two hours before the sun went down. "We entered a vast plain, and two or three hours before day we crossed the Araxes by a bridge of three arches. Coming in sight of the ruins, we waited for day. I lay down upon the bare ground, but it was too cold to sleep."

(Perhaps he was tired after riding through the night, or his mind was still on translation work, but the river was not the Araxes; this river lies some thousand miles to the north of where he was. The bridge they crossed on their way from Shiraz to Persepolis was over the river Kur Rud.)

As soon as the sun rose Henry was eager to reach the ruins, filled with curiosity and anticipation. It was with amazement he noticed the complete lack of interest displayed by the rest of his company. Perhaps, living as near as they did to Persepolis, it was a case of familiarity breeding contempt; but they had not the slightest inclination to look at this ancient place. From the moment they climbed the great terrace they all lay down and fell asleep.

They, for their part, could not understand why people should come from far away to look at nothing but ruins. One of the servants stayed awake long enough to say to Henry, "A nice place, Sahib. Good air and a fine garden; you may carry brandy and drink here at leisure!" Poor man. Expressing his idea of human happiness, he could only suppose that his master's whole purpose in making the journey to Persepolis was to have a drinking bout.

But for Henry, as he wandered alone among the remains of antiquity, his mind was filled with visions of the past—the banquets, the revelries, and the songs that had echoed over the surrounding mountains.

He gazed up at the huge columns still standing sentinel, pointing ever upward like accusing fingers, their capitals almost as long as the shafts.

There was a certain awe in looking out over the plains beyond which, in ancient Babylon, Nebuchadnezzar set up his great image of gold. Did Henry fancy he could hear that vast orchestra with its sound of the dulcimer, flute, and harps commanding the people to bow down and worship the great king (Daniel 3)?

Here was the place where Daniel, the chief-president of Darius, may have come with his king to the festivals, walking over these same flagstones (Daniel 6).

As this earnest student of the Scriptures walked around, many more of the names in the Old Testament history must have come vividly alive in his alert mind.

For generation after generation Persepolis had been the palace of kings, symbol of might and majesty—until that day when Alexander came marching with his Greek army to force their way through the band of defending tribesmen, burning it to ashes.

Now all was silent and austere, hiding its secrets as if in shame.

The time had gone all too quickly and Henry realized that the sun was going down on yet another day. Soon it would be necessary to prepare for the return journey back to Shiraz.

He rode on into the next village to get a meal before rejoining his servants and the two guards. Then, rousing those who still wanted to sleep, they were ready to start for Shiraz.

On the return journey the company lost their way. They were not willing to be guided by Henry, who insisted that he remembered the way they had come and stressed that they were taking the wrong road.

Mile after mile they rode until they came across a group of villagers spending the night on their threshingfloor in the field; they now asked for directions. To the astonishment of everyone but Henry, they were told to go back to the way which he had first suggested.

Now they were so impressed with his geographical skill that when it was time for them to stop for prayers they asked him to point the way. "After setting their faces toward Mecca, as nearly as I could, I went and sat down on the margin near the bridge. Here the water falling over some fragments of the bridge under the arches produced a roar which, contrasting with the stillness all around, had a grand effect. Here I thought again of the multitudes who had once pursued their labors and pleasures on its banks."

Of all the wide experiences of Henry's life in various parts of the world, he appreciated most the quiet calm of sitting beside a stream in a pleasant place or listening to the happy roar of a waterfall, prizing, as he did, the moments when he could draw aside from everything and be alone. "Be still and know that I am God" must have been a favorite verse.

As soon as the Muslims had finished their prayers, Henry rejoined the group and mounted his horse. Not wishing to reach Shiraz before the gates were opened, they stayed at a caravanserai (inn) on the way. "I put my head into a poor corner and slept soundly upon the hard stone." Obviously this was not a four-star hotel!

The visit had not been without its value for it gave Henry the opportunity for discussion with the guards, who asked questions as they rode.

"What think you of Christ?" one asked.

"The same as you say—the Word of God."

"Was He a Prophet?"

"Yes . . . but what it chiefly concerns us to know is He was an atonement for the sins of men." This time the man made no reply.

CHAPTER **23**

COMPLETING THE TASK

During his months in Shiraz Henry was often involved in controversial discussions, boldly seeking every opportunity to show Christ to the people of Persia, while he worked incessantly to produce the New Testament in their language.

On Christmas Day he arranged a party for some Armenian friends and, at Jaffir Ali's request, he invited a Sufi master and his disciples. He had hoped there would be some helpful conversation but in this he was disappointed. Although Seid Ali made an attempt to open this by explaining the meaning of the Lord's Supper, the Sufis remained silent. The subject had to be dropped as the meal was ready, and the moment it was over the guests rose to leave.

On February 14, 1812, the New Testament was completed; three weeks later the translation of the book of Psalms was also finished. "A sweet employment caused six weary moons that waxed and waned since the commencement to pass unnoticed."

Scribes were employed to prepare two special volumes, one to be presented to the Shah and the other to his son, Prince Abbas Mirza. Three months later these two manuscripts were finished.

It was usual for a Persian writer to present his work to the Shah for his approval before being published. Henry not only felt it a matter of courtesy to follow the Persian custom; he also realized that the Shah's opinion could have a vital effect on the readers he was aiming for.

Since there was no one except Henry who could take charge of the precious books and deliver them to Tehran, he decided to take them himself and present them in person.

All that remained for him to do in Shiraz was to supervise the making of several copies of the script. This left him free to spend time with Seid and Jaffir Ali, reading to them at their request portions of the Old Testament. Their interest and friendliness had been a great support during his stay in their city, and he was grateful.

On their last day together, Seid Ali was given instructions of what to do with the manuscripts in the event of Henry's death;

some were to be sent to India for printing by the Serampore Press. The two royal copies were wrapped carefully, ready to be taken by Henry for correction during his journey to Tehran.

Although Henry's health had improved since leaving the ferocious heat of the Indian summer, he was still troubled with chest pains, particularly after any long conversation or dispute. His will and determination to succeed in the work to which, under God, he had set his hand was far stronger then the frail frame in which they were housed.

He felt an increasing urgency to complete whatever tasks lay ahead in Persia. He realized that the wisest plan would be to go straight home to England, where he could regain his strength before returning to his work in India.

Had he been blessed with a wife at this stage it is likely she would have urged him to be reasonable and do just that. There were, in fact, days when he felt so unwell he almost decided to go back to Bushire and get a ship there. But his mind was set on personally handing over the precious Persian translation into the hands of the Shah. Only when that part of his mission was completed could he feel free to turn his face toward home, and hopeful recovery.

Some may be inclined to call this pride, but a more charitable explanation would be that he feared, with robbers and bandits so prevalent, that his years' work might be destroyed.

In one of his long letters to Corrie, his friend in India, Henry wrote, "I can think of no greater happiness than to be settled for life in India, superintending schools as we did."

But for the moment it was necessary to prepare for the journey to Tehran. He was pleased that his party was to include the Rev. William Canning, on his way to the British Embassy in Tehran as the new chaplain.

This time there was no trumpeter to announce his departure, and with mixed feelings Henry mounted his horse to ride north across the great Persian plateau toward Tehran.

Chapter 24

JOURNEY TO TEHRAN

The travelers left Shiraz in the evening and were passing Persepolis, place of memories, about ten hours later. On May thirteenth they stopped for the day at a caravanserai, where Henry used the time to start correcting his manuscript until it was time to continue the journey.

The way led through mountainous country, bare except for heather and broom, with little protection from the gusty, cold wind. At one point there was a hoarfrost and ice in the puddles, and away in the distance the high ridges were covered in snow.

It was May twenty-second when they arrived at Isfahan—a beautiful city of minarets, domes, and pigeon towers, and sparkling fountains playing in the shade of many trees. Henry and Canning, as foreigners of some importance, were accommodated comfortably in one of the Shah's palaces. Here Henry was pleased to meet his old Shiraz scribe who willingly helped him go through the manuscript until they had finished the corrections. Now it was ready for presentation.

They left Isfahan at the end of the month, traveling through attractive countryside with many trees, cornfields, and running streams. "It was the first place I have seen in Asia which exhibited anything of the scenery of England. It was a mild, moonlit night and a nightingale filled the whole valley with his notes."

Night after night they pressed on, staying some days for rest. They were often chatting with the villagers who gathered round in their eagerness to talk with the European in their midst, who spoke to them so confidently of his faith in Jesus Christ.

The company neared Tehran on June eighth, before the gates were open. Henry put his bed down on the high road outside the walls and slept. He woke with the dawn and drew his coat closer round him, for the morning air was sharp. With half-closed eyes he looked at the wall against which he lay, wondering where he was, until his thoughts cleared. This was Tehran, another step toward his goal. Here he hoped to obtain an introduction from the British Ambassador, for without this he would not be allowed to approach the Shah.

To his intense dismay Henry found that the Ambassador, Sir Gore Ouseley, was away at his home in Tabriz, about 400 miles further north and west. Desperately he began to consider what steps he could take for gaining an audience with the Shah and Prince. He was anxious to lose no time in presenting his book.

Henry learned that the Shah's Prime Minister, Mirza Shufi, was at the camp at Karaj, a night's journey further on. Fortunately, Jaffir Ali had given him a letter of introduction to the Premier. It was thus decided that he should go on alone to Karaj and present it to Mirza Shufi, seeking his assistance in arranging a meeting with the Shah.

Henry waited till evening to set off and on arrival at a caravanserai near to the camp he sent a messenger to take Jaffir Ali's letter to the Premier. When Henry was sent for he found Mirza Shufi lying on the verandah of the Shah's tent of audience.

With him were two officials who took little notice of the newcomer, not rising as was their custom nor offering the usual water-pipe. However, when they learned the object of his visit their tongues were loosened and they began a controversial discussion on religion and metaphysics that continued for two hours.

"He speaks good Persian," was the final comment and Henry knew he was no nearer to gaining permission to meet the

Shah than he had been before. In despair he returned to his lodging.

While he stayed on at Karaj, guarding his precious manuscript, hoping against hope that the Shah might come there and he would be given an audience, Henry was invited to attend the Premier's assembly. This time he took his book with him.

He found himself surrounded by a group of scholars intent on disproving his Christian faith. He sat alone among the hostile Mullahs. After a lengthy, controversial, and noisy dispute, the Premier, who had set the whole thing in motion, challenged the frail but valiant defender of the faith: "You had better say God is God, and Muhammad is the prophet of God."

Squaring his shoulders to meet the anticipated opposition, Henry replied, "God is God, and Jesus is the Son of God."

Immediately there was an angry tumult and one of them said, "What will you say when your tongue is burnt out for this blasphemy?"

As Mirza Shufi rose to leave, followed by the rest of the group, Henry saw his book lying on the floor, in danger of being trampled on. Quickly he went to retrieve it and wrapped it carefully in a towel, "while they looked at me with supreme contempt. Thus I walked alone to my tent, to pass the rest of the day in heat and dirt."

To complete the day of frustration and denouncement, Henry received a message from the Premier that evening to the effect that he could not, or would not, arrange for the Englishman to meet the Shah or Prince Abbas Mirza.

The only thing to do now was to press on and try to reach the Ambassador at Tabriz. Mr. Canning, the chaplain on his way to the Embassy, who had stayed behind at Tehran, now rejoined Henry. Together they started on their journey to Tabriz, covering some forty miles before they stopped at a village.

"As I sat down in the dust on the shady side of a walled village and surveyed the plains over which our road lay, I sighed at the thoughts of my dear friends in India and England, of the vast regions I must travel before I can get to either, and of the various hindrances which present themselves to my going forward. I comfort myself with the hope that God has something for me to do by thus delaying my exit."

Only someone who has found himself many difficult miles away from home and friends, with little prospect of a likely return, could appreciate the depth of Henry's feelings at this time.

They were further delayed by the sudden illness of Canning and were unable to leave the village until June sixteenth. Then, warmly wrapped against the cold north wind blowing in from the Caspian Sea, they reached Zanjan. Here they were heartened by the sudden possibility of a

cup of tea! Among the merchants bringing goods from Tehran were two Tartars
carrying iron and tea for sale. Seeing the
chance of a sale they approached Henry.
"Do you want tea of Cathay?" they asked.
Indeed he did! Much to their disappointment
they found the merchants could really
speak nothing but Turkish; any negotia-
tions with them proved so difficult that
the blissful cup never materialized.

As they progressed the whole company
was plagued with recurring bouts of fever,
headaches, and fatigue, with Henry relaps-
ing several times and quite unable to move
on. Lack of sleep, lack of refreshment,
exposure to the sun, and alternating cold
winds drained his strength until, hardly
able to sit his horse, Henry at last reached
the gates of Tabriz. With his little remain-
ing breath, he asked a man to take him to
the Ambassador's house.

CHAPTER 25

CONVALESCENCE

The list of ministerial duties of an ambassador is not likely to include that of taking into the embassy residence a sick missionary translator on his way to seek audience with the royal monarch. But to their lasting credit, Sir Gore Ouseley and his wife took up the challenge facing them.

The man who had arrived on their doorstep in a state of collapse was the clergyman they had already met while staying at Shiraz—the one who had preached to their household and baptized their child. Now he was desperately ill and in need of all the love and care available, a servant of God to be nursed back to health.

For many days Henry was barely conscious as he lay in a raging fever; but in lucid moments he was acutely aware of the kind attention he was being given by the

Ambassador and his wife.

It would seem like a touch of irony that during his illness the Prince Abbas Shiraz came on a visit to the house. What an opportunity to present him with his copy of the manuscript—one of the main objects of Henry's journey. But this was not possible. The sick man was delirious, and unable to lift his head from the pillow.

Some weeks later the fever responded to the excellent nursing, and gradually the invalid began to improve. Once again, with recovery, Henry's inherent good spirits revived. During convalescence his infectious laugh was heard again, this time throughout the Embassy, as he romped with the child of the house. She had quickly found a way into his heart.

He was reminded of the happy times he had spent with the orphan child who shared her treasures with him in the home of Mrs. Sherwood in India, and of the fun he had enjoyed with the children of David Brown on the lawn at Aldeen.

Like many people, he found that happiness and laughter can do more for a convalescent than strong medicine.

A letter from Lydia had at last reached Henry during his illness, and now he was sufficiently recovered to be able to reply. In August he wrote, "It has pleased God to restore me to life and health again. Not that I have recovered my former strength, but I consider myself sufficiently restored to proceed with my journey. My daily prayer is that my late chastisement may have its intended effect, and make me all the rest of my days more humble and less self-confident. . . . In prayer Christ appears to me my life and strength; but at other times I am as thoughtless and bold as if I had all life and strength in myself. . . . An account of all my discussions with these mystic philosophers must be reserved to the time of our meeting. Do I dream, do I venture to think and write of such an event as that? Is it possible that we shall ever meet again below? Though it is possible, I dare not indulge such a pleasing hope yet. . . ."

At last Henry was forced to the realization that he must abandon his plan of presenting his book to the Shah. His journey must now be homeward if he was ever to reach England. He discussed the matter with Sir Gore and Lady Ouseley, deeply regretting the fact that he had not been able to complete his mission. His disappointment was somewhat eased by the kindness of his host, who promised to take charge of the New Testament translation until he could hand it over personally to the Shah and the Prince. (When later this promise was fulfilled the Shah was delighted and publicly expressed his approval, commending it as a book to be read from beginning to end.)

While still at the Embassy, Henry wrote to his well-loved old friend and counselor,

Simeon, at Cambridge. Henry told him of the proposed furlough, hoping he would understand how necessary this was.

Henry was, of course, still holding the position of a chaplain with the East India Company so, with his usual courteous attention to protocol, he sent a letter to Mr. Charles Grant. He asked that the sick leave should be extended in order that he could go home to England before returning once more to India.

The strings of home were beginning to pull stronger than ever and Henry determined to start on his long journey as soon as possible. From Tabriz he would need to travel across country, through Turkey, to Constantinople (modern Istanbul).

The Ouseleys were concerned that he should so soon contemplate the daunting prospect of traveling alone, except for servants, over 1,300 miles of harsh and often hostile country; it was something even a robust person would view with apprehension. Unfortunately, they could see that their warnings were falling on deaf ears. Henry had become obsessed with the idea of returning to England by the shortest route, even though it was more hazardous for a sick man.

Not being able to persuade him to stay longer, the Ambassador and his wife did their best to send him on his way as well-prepared as possible. Sir Gore arranged for especially strong Chappar horses to be provided for the whole journey and gave Henry letters of introduction to the various governors of the land over which he would travel. He also wrote one for the British Ambassador at Constantinople. He planned with Henry the route through Armenia and Turkey, knowing this would be the safest one and possibly less likely to be attacked by bandits.

Henry would need to take with him Armenian servants who knew both the Persian and Turkish languages, and he managed to find one, Antoine, as a groom. Henry employed Sergius, who professed to know Persian, as an interpreter.

On September 2, 1812, Henry waved goodbye to his hosts and set his face westward toward the "royal road" of ancient Persia. Along this way had traveled many great kings from the past.

It was not long before he found that his interpreter's knowledge of Persian was "rather scanty," so conversation was limited. Undaunted, Henry records, "We rode silently along. For my part, I could not have enjoyed any companion so much as I did my own feelings." He had much to occupy his mind: fears, frustrated hopes, regrets, and unfulfilled longings.

CHAPTER 26

TOWARDS HOME

Once out of the city of Tabriz, with its many mosques, domes, lakes, and noisy bazaars, they came out onto the plain. This stretches for many miles, enclosed by remote, silent mountains whose summits merge with the blue heavens. Because of his long illness Henry appreciated more than ever—with a joyful sense of gratitude— the beauty and grandeur which he saw as he and Sergius rode along.

Toward the northwest edge of the plain, they came to Sofian, looking for their pre-arranged accommodation in the attractive garden village. They found the farmer in his field directing his laborers, who were cutting straw into fine pieces to be made into fodder for the cattle. Henry watched with interest as they drew over the straw a cylinder fitted with triangular plates.

The farmer seemed too busy to pay attention to his visitors but sent one of his men to show Henry the place where he was to sleep. The offered room turned out to be unsatisfactory—a room with only three walls. On requesting one with four walls, Henry was taken to a weaver's house where "notwithstanding the mosquitoes and other vermin, I passed the night comfortably enough."

It was very hot the next day as they went through a mountain pass, but to relieve the tediousness of the way, Henry was able to dismount. He sat thankfully beside a brook to eat his picnic of bread and raisins and, cupping his hands, took a cooling drink from the mountain stream.

His next bedroom was a corner in a stable, partitioned off for privacy—but not from the strong smell of the horses. It was a healthy smell, he had always been told!

As he sat ruminating over the past day's happenings he reproached himself, feeling he had been too impatient with his servants over some trifling irritation. "How much more noble and God-like to bear with calmness and observe with pity, rather than anger, the failings and offences of others!"

While he had pity for others, Henry had little for himself—undertaking what must have been a nightmare journey, with its lack of all comfort, enduring so many inconveniences and trials. In all his travels in various parts of the world his fastidious mind never lost its natural instinct for the cultured way of life; but this had been included in the sacrifice when, in Cambridge all those years before, he had given up the prospect of a professional academic career. It is difficult to appreciate what it cost him to do without even the most basic amenities.

Today the tourist sleeps in a comfortable room with hot and cold water, eats a substantial meal in a softly lit dining room, driving on next day in his high-powered car to the next smart hotel. He still finds an excuse to grumble! And should it be necessary, he can board a plane to fly him straight home. In 1812 there were no such luxuries.

By September sixth the company arrived at the banks of the Araxes, a river "broad as the Isis, with a current as strong as that of the Ganges." The ferryboat, in appearance something like a large fish, was tied up on the opposite side so, not knowing how long it would be before it came across, Henry decided to catch up with his sleep.

But finding his servants had the same idea and that it was possible no one would be awake when the ferryman came, he roused himself to keep on watch. In fact, it was dawn before the ferry came over, the man pushing it with a stick.

"I dare say he had never seen or heard of an oar, but we arrived safely on the other side in about two minutes."

At Nackshan it was difficult to find a lodging; but eventually one man, an important citizen, offered the use of his washhouse, and a corner was cleaned and made ready for Henry's bedroom.

By this time it was almost noon and Henry's baggage had not yet caught up with them, so he had to go without breakfast. But he was so tired that, hungry as he was, he slept till the afternoon.

On the next lap, Henry the linguist was hardly conscious of the miles, his mind completely taken up with a Hebrew word in the 16th Psalm which, he said, led him gradually into speculations on the eighth conjugation of the Arabic verb! "I am glad that my philological curiosity is revived as my mind will be less liable to idleness."

Next they came within sight of a high mountain, and Henry was excited to learn that this was Ararat. Immediately his thoughts flew back to the Old Testament story, wondering on which spot Noah built his altar and offered his first thanksgiving sacrifice.

In the surrounding countryside there was abundant evidence of God's promise that planting and harvest should not cease. "I had not seen such fertility in any part of the Shah's dominions."

The next night the company lost their way, finding themselves in an area with many flooded ditches, which in the darkness were difficult to see and avoid. The horse carrying luggage sank in one so deep that the water soaked the contents of the bags, including Henry's books.

It was hopeless to try and find the next halting place in the dark, so they tried to get help at a village they happened upon. For some time they wandered round without success, eventually knocking at a door where they were greeted by two silver-haired, elderly men. These men invited Henry in and he explained that they were lost, traveling toward the Turkish border. Although it was late these good Samaritans lit a fire to dry their guest and his books, offering hot coffee and a shelter for the rest of the night.

At daylight, with the help of a man from the village, they were guided through grass and mire to the mountain pass which they found led to country as dry as the last one was wet. They were now quite near to Mount Ararat, and soon arrived at Erivan.

Chapter 27

POMP AND CEREMONY

Henry made his way to the Governor's palatial residence at Erivan. Hosyn Khan, who commanded this highly important fortress on the frontier, was well aware of his own importance. When the visitor was summoned to his presence, Hosyn went on reading his Koran for several minutes before exchanging greetings. When the pleasantries were over he resumed his devotions, giving Henry the opportunity to admire the splendor of his surroundings.

The Governor was wearing a magnificent shawl-dress but he ceremoniously exchanged this for a still richer pelisse, pretending to feel cold. He looked in good health but, seemingly to display the fact that he had a physician in residence, called for him to attend and feel his pulse. Once this had been done, the doctor took his place with the brightly-dressed servants standing to one side.

The letter of introduction Henry had brought had not been opened but lay on the floor until a moonshee was called to open and read it. Then Hosyn Khan became interested and attentive as he listened to what Sir Gore Ouseley had written about the translations. His visitor was a man of more importance than he had supposed. From then on one of the Governor's lieutenants was ordered to look after him.

During the afternoon Henry was asked to come again to the Governor's house. This time he found Hosyn reclining on a couch near a sparkling fountain which was set in a basin of white marble and contained grapes and melons. From far below the window came the pleasant murmur of a stream bubbling over stones and running on through the lovely gardens, behind which Henry caught sight of Mt. Ararat once again.

This time Hosyn Khan was entirely free of ceremony, and although Henry tried to draw him into conversation he seemed too languid even to talk. But at the end of the session the Khan was not too fatigued to order a guard and fresh horses for the journey which would eventually take Henry across Turkey.

The next-calling place was Etschmiadzin, religious capital of the Armenians since 300 A.D. With his letter of introduction Henry went to his lodging, an Armenian monastery where the monks take no vows but that of celibacy. One of the monks named Serope, a linguist who spoke French and Italian as well as English, took Henry to the room appointed for him. The monk was keen to tell Henry the fascinating story of his life. This monk was endeavoring to set up a college to teach the young Armenians logic, rhetoric and other sciences. With that accomplished he planned to retire to India and there write and print religious works in Armenian. "I said all I could to encourage him in such a blessed work, promising him every aid from the English." When the bells rang for vespers they went together into the church.

The next day Henry had an interview with the Abbot, who welcomed him warmly and told him to consider himself completely at home in the monastery. The attention and kindness of the community had been so overwhelming and the grateful traveler was so happy to be there that, Henry said, duty permitting, he could almost be willing to become a monk himself. "[The Abbot] smiled and, fearing perhaps that I was in earnest, said that they had quite enough!"

During Henry's stay the kind Serope proved to be the perfect host, doing all he could to make his guest comfortable. Then he helped Henry in his preparations for the journey ahead, advising him on the mode of travel in Turkey.

Much of the expensive equipment Henry

had brought from Tabriz would have to be discarded, including a portable table and chair and a supply of sugar. Although this was in an age long before the advent of airplanes and airlines, there was nevertheless a restriction on the weight of luggage that could be carried. All the necessities had to be transferred from the heavy trunk and packed into bags, and a sword was bought for protection against robbers. Henry's servant was also armed.

The kindness and brotherly fellowship Henry had received at the monastery put new vigor into him and sent him on his way with fresh hope of success in his struggle to reach first Constantinople, then his beloved Cornwall, and eventually to return to India, hopefully bringing Lydia with him.

They left the monastery on September seventeenth. The first night the guard was able to find a comfortable lodging and at dawn Henry was ready to move on. After three hours' riding they had left the plain of Ararat behind.

When they again reached the Araxes Henry let the company go on while he stayed to have a quick dip in the river—the last opportunity he would have of bathing in Persian waters. Soon afterwards they came to a village where the headman was sitting in a shed reading his Koran, with his sword, rifle, and pistol at his side. He was friendly and spoke to them in Persian;

but he chanted in Arabic with equal fluency.

The next stage of the journey took them along a dangerously steep road over the mountains which led to many miles of tedious tableland. It was hot and airless, and nothing could be seen but bare rock.

At last they came to an Armenian village in a hollow. The place looked strange with conical piles of peat everywhere, which the villagers used for their fires when they had no wood. All around were fields of growing grain.

The travelers were now over the border and had left Persia for the domains of the Sultan of Turkey. This was the first Turkish village. "Not a Persian cap to be seen; the respectable people wore a red Turkish cap."

CHAPTER **28**

THE LAST RIDE

I n the next village, Henry found himself lodged in a room that was a thoroughfare for horses, cows, buffalo, and sheep. The animals took little notice of the man in their midst—but most of the local people came to stand and stare!

The guards were ever on the alert as they traveled over the solitary plains, and when they came in sight of a castle on a hilltop they moved with great caution. On investigation it turned out to be quite empty—still and silent as the grave—and they went on.

The next alarm came when they saw a company of men in a valley, and the guards again took their place in front, guns at the ready. They realized there was nothing to fear when they saw carts and oxen; but the men in the valley were not so sure that Henry's party were not bandits.

They prepared to fire, but eventually understood that there was no danger. They proved to be an innocent group of Armenians carrying wood from the town of Kars, to burn with peat on their home fires.

When they reached Kars Henry was surprised to see its European appearance; with houses of stone, carts passing along the streets, a fort set high on a hill, and an enormous cemetery.

His groom took him at once to the Governor. Provided for him in an Armenian's house was an excellent room, which had bow windows complete with cushioned seats, and a wide view of the fort and river. The Governor sent a message saying that he would be pleased for Henry to stay a few days and when he was ready to go on there would be horses and guards supplied.

When the day came, there was only one guard available, a Tartar who quickly displayed his fierce character by flogging the baggage-horse until it fell with its load. While this was being sorted out a crowd gathered—curiosity being the same the world over. When the horse was once more on its feet, they turned their attention on the stranger and his unusual clothing. But it appeared to be his Russian boots that interested them most of all!

The tuberculosis Henry had been fighting for so long was beginning to take its toll on his weakened body, and before they reached their next stopping place he was ill, with a high temperature. Hassan, the Tartar, went ahead and procured a room with a fire. Here the invalid would have been very comfortable, had it not been that Hassan decided to share it with him.

Drawn by the warmth of the fire in contrast to the frost outside, other people joined them while waiting for the time of the meal. They were fascinated by Henry's watch and could not resist asking every few minutes, "Sir, what is your timer telling us now?"

The next day Henry was sufficiently recovered to be able to continue. The journey led through a beautiful forest of tall firs, with clear streams running in the valleys and lofty trees crowning the surrounding hills. Smooth paths led into the secret depths of the dark wood, and over all there was a solitude that brought tranquility to the mind. After nine hours of riding through these peaceful scenes they arrived at the post-house. Here Henry found for himself quarters in the stable-room, thus avoiding the intrusion of Hassan, and at last was able to sleep in quiet.

The following morning the road brought them to a hot spring which ran into a pool. The pool itself was set within four porches, beneath semi-circular arches, reminding Henry of the healing pool of Bethesda (John 5:2).

At this pleasant spot the company halted and stayed long enough for a bath. Hassan, who knew well enough how to make life enjoyable for himself, smoked his calean (water-pipe) while up to his chin in water!

At Erzurum they found crowded streets and shops against a background of bougainvillaea and trailing vines. The crowds viewed with curiosity the strange assortment of newcomers, particularly the thin, frail rider with the white face. From his Persian attendants and the lower part of his clothing he would appear to be Persian; but there was something about him that stamped him as European.

When they realized that these were no more than peaceful travelers, the natural Turkish generosity came to the fore. They brought melons and other food, offering them to the strangers with a dignified bow.

Everything emphasized for Henry the fact that he was in a Turkish town for the first time. "The red cap, stateliness, and rich dress and variety of turbans was realized as I had seen it in pictures."

As they left Erzurum his temperature again rose. He was unable to eat or to drink anything but weak tea.

But even in his low state he recorded in his journal, "My soul rests in Him who is as an anchor of the soul, sure and steadfast, which though not seen, keeps me fast."

Mile after mile the hazardous journey continued, with Henry often near to collapse. Realizing the serious state of his health, he was desperate to complete his journey, but the merciless Hassan set the pace each day according to his own whim. Sometimes he would race the horses as if in a chariot contest, and another time delay procedure by refusing to get up until late in the day.

Sometimes he would not exert himself to find a room for Henry, who had then to depend on his servant Sergius.

In one stable-room Henry was so ill that he tried to get relief by laying his aching head down among the baggage on the damp floor before he lost consciousness. One can only wonder how he survived at all; yet he was able to write in his journal the next morning: "Preserving mercy made me see the light of another day. The sleep had refreshed me but I was feeble and shaken. Yet the merciless Hassan hurried me on."

At one lodging there were two Persian fellow-travelers who saw Henry's distress and went to his assistance. Meanwhile Hassan stood in complete indifference— except to complain of the delay the illness would cause.

Then came the morning when there were no horses ready, giving Henry a brief respite. "I sat in the orchard and thought with sweet comfort and peace of my God—in solitude my company, my friend, and my comforter. When shall time give place to eternity? When appears that new heaven and new earth wherein dwells righteousness . . . none of those corrup-

tions which add still more to the miseries
of mortality shall be seen or heard of any
more."

For the last time the journal had recorded
the thoughts of this dying man, and the book
was closed—to be opened only much later
by his sorrowing friends in an atmosphere
of reverent awe and wonder.

Henry Martyn had ridden himself to
death. There is no record of the last ten days
of his life, but it is known that he reached
Tokat—either still holding the reins of his
horse or, more likely, by being carried
there. In Tokat, on October 16, 1812, his old
complaint, tuberculosis, possibly combined
with whatever plague happened to be raging at the time, released his spirit from its
battered shell. He was only thirty-one
years old.

There may not have been a friendly hand
for him to hold as he entered the valley of
the shadow, but the trumpets must have
sounded as the gates of the Celestial City
swung open to receive this faithful servant
of the God he worshiped.

Henry had left instructions with
Sergius to take all the papers and personal
belongings on with him to the British
Embassy at Constantinople. In February of
the following year, Charles Simeon heard
from the Ambassador's secretary, Isaac
Morier, that an Armenian servant named
Sergius had come into the office. He had
brought the journal and other effects of

his master, Henry Martyn, and reported that his master had died at Tokat on or about October 16 and had been given Christian burial by the Armenians.

The sorrowing Simeon wrote to Calcutta to let his friends there know of Henry's death, and Lydia was also informed.

So the work of Henry Martyn was ended, and a humble grave in a foreign country was all the world could offer him.

CHAPTER 29

TO WHOM TRIBUTE IS DUE

I n every way Henry Martyn was outstanding. In his faith there was the simple trust of a child and the greatness of a giant— all enfolded in a meek humility and an awesome reverence. He was brilliant as a scholar, naive as an individual, solemn in judgment but merry in laughter. He had a love for people and crowds, as well as a taste for solitude.

His writings have inspired many to aim for the highest standard in their work for God. Great men such as Murray McCheyne and Andrew Bonar, famous ministers of the Church of Scotland, read the memoirs of Martyn in the early part of their ministry and recorded in their diaries the great impact this had on them.

Who can tell how many more have been

influenced by his life and work? The mystics of Islam, his many friends and colleagues, and subsequent generations in many lands all owe him a tremendous debt.

Moreover, he was one of the Church's greatest linguists. He was responsible for translating the whole of the New Testament and the Prayer Book into Hindustani (Urdu), and for translating the Psalms of David and the New Testament into Persian. Indeed, until recently his Urdu New Testament was the only major translation available, although it has been extensively revised over the years.

A present-day missionary to Urdu-speaking Muslims in Pakistan, Vivienne Stacey, quotes Canon W. J. Edmonds' tribute to Henry Martyn: "I know no parallel to these achievements of Henry Martyn . . . the born translator. He masters grammar, observes idioms, accumulates vocabulary, reads and listens, corrects and even reconstructs. Above all, he prays. He lives in the Spirit and rises from his knees full of the mind of the Spirit."

The papers and the first part of Henry's journal, which he had left with his friend Daniel Corrie in India, were sent to his executors, Charles Simeon and John Thornton. The latter section of the journal and the letters written when he was in Persia and Turkey were sent on by Morier from Constantinople. With a deepening sense of awe these were studied carefully in Simeon's room at Cambridge. In 1819 the journal and some letters were faithfully reproduced by John Sargeant.

The first edition of Henry Martyn's translation into Persian was printed in St. Petersburg (Leningrad) in 1815 by the Russian Bible Society. For the second edition, printed by the Serampore Press, Seid Ali of Shiraz was invited to Calcutta in 1816 to supervise the actual printing.

Lydia, at last freed from the decision-making with which she seemed unable to cope, continued to live at Marazion for a further seventeen years—quietly mourning the memory of the man she had loved, but never married. She was ill for several years with cancer and died in 1829 at the age of fifty-four.

Henry Martyn is remembered in his native Cornwall, and the baptistry in Truro Cathedral is regarded as his memorial. On Market Street, Cambridge, stands the Henry Martyn Hall—next to Holy Trinity Church where Henry was at one time curate for Charles Simeon. Around the walls of the hall are the names of subsequent Cambridge graduates who followed Henry's example in taking the gospel overseas; in the same building a library and an experienced adviser are on hand for the benefit of those considering the same step today.

A portrait of Henry, which was painted in Calcutta in 1810 before he left for Persia, was sent as a gift to Simeon and he received it in 1812. In 1836 it was bequeathed to Cambridge University Library, and the portrait is now on loan to the Henry Martyn Hall. There is a copy of it in St. John's College Library, reminding today's students of the Cambridge man who in his day was winner of 1st Smith's prize and Senior Wrangler.

Above all his achievements, however, Henry Martyn was a man longing for God, always striving to enter in at the gate of every Christian experience, thirsting after righteousness, critical of his own weakness, deploring what he felt to be his lack of holy living.

Although Henry Martyn's life on earth has ended, the results of his faithful ministry continue through the years. The memory of his courage, endurance, and dedication must present a lasting challenge to all Christian people.

BIBLIOGRAPHY

Bentley-Taylor, D., *My Love Must Wait*

Colebrooke, T. E., *Life of Mountstuart Elphinstone*

Cook, J. M., *The Persian Empire*

Dicks, Brian, *The Ancient Persians*

Loane, Marcus, *Cambridge and the Evangelical Succession*

Padwick, Constance, *Henry Martyn— Confessor of the Faith*

Sargeant, John, *The Life and Letters of Henry Martyn*

Smith, George, LLD, *Henry Martyn, Saint and Scholar*

Stacey, Vivienne, *Life of Henry Martyn*

Ure, John, *The Trail of Tamerlane*

Wood, Philip, *Touring Iran*

I am also indebted to:

the Very Rev. D. J. Shearlock, Dean of
    Truro Cathedral

Mr. S. M. Mischler, former Headmaster
    at Cathedral School, Truro

Mr. H. L. Douch, BA, Curator of Truro
    Museum and Art Gallery

the Library of St. John's College,
    Cambridge

Leicester University

Leicester Reference Library

the Church Missionary Society

Serampore College, Calcutta

the Rev. John Kirkby, BD, BSc, Rector of
    St. Mary's Church, Byfleet, Surrey

and the Rev. Canon D. W. Gundry, BD,
    MTh, Canon Chancellor of Leicester
    Cathedral

By the same author:

WILLIAM CAREY: BY TRADE A COBBLER

This book was produced by the Christian Literature Crusade. We hope it has been helpful to you in living the Christian life. CLC is a literature mission with ministry in over 45 countries worldwide. If you would like to know more about us, or are interested in opportunities to serve with a faith mission, we invite you to write to:

Christian Literature Crusade
P.O. Box 1449
Fort Washington, PA 19034